How Many Times Do I Forgive?

LIFE-CHANGING STORIES OF PEOPLE WHO
HAVE CHOSEN TO FORGIVE

Gloria Ewing Lockhart

TRILOGY CHRISTIAN PUBLISHERS

Tustin, CA

Trilogy Christian Publishers

A Wholly Owned Subsidiary of Trinity Broadcasting Network

2442 Michelle Drive

Tustin, CA 92780

For information, address Trilogy Christian Publishing

Rights Department, 2442 Michelle Drive, Tustin, Ca 92780.

Trilogy Christian Publishing/ TBN and colophon are trademarks of Trinity Broadcasting Network.

For information about special discounts for bulk purchases, please contact Trilogy Christian Publishing.

Manufactured in the United States of America

10 9 8 7 6 5 4 3 2 1

Library of Congress Cataloging-in-Publication Data is available.

ISBN 978-1-64088-227-0

ISBN 978-1-64088-228-7 (ebook)

Contents

Dedication

To anyone having a hard time forgiving others or being forgiven, please read the stories in this book with an open heart.

To anyone who has already followed the path of forgiveness, and are thriving in God's goodness, please share these stories with those who are reluctant to forgive. Let the stories encourage them and support them, but most importantly, allow them to know God's promise: "For I know the plans I have for you, declares the Lord, plans to prosper you and not to harm you, plans to give you hope and a future" (Jeremiah 29:11 NIV).

Acknowledgements

Forty-three years ago, I climbed Mt. Kilimanjaro. Writing this book recalled that remarkable ascent. Like that trek, it would have been impossible without so many people who helped and encouraged me. My success then, like my success now, depended on wonderful people, and God's grace.

From the beginning of time, God pronounced that I would author this book. You had my future already planned. "You saw me before I was born. Every day of my life was recorded in your book. Every moment was laid out before a single day had passed" (Psalm 139:16 NLT). I'm deeply grateful to have Your calling on my life. As I would write, You would reveal the importance of how this book would heal those on their journey of forgiveness.

My family, I love you more than I can say. My loving daughter, Tiombe, your words inspired me to "Just keep it moving." My siblings have stood by me and believed in my many projects: Eva Clark, Lydia Ewing, and Sylvette Twiggs.

Other amazing extended family, you encouraged and empowered me in each stage of the journey. I am grateful.

Trilogy Christian Publishing, affiliate of TBN, you embraced my mission and pushed me beyond limits. Thank you for keeping me focused and inspired with words of wisdom. You'd say, "You're almost there, the Lord has great plans for your work."

My many donors, thank you for backing this project: Vic and Donetta Serafini, Gary Foster, Earl and Louise Butler, William and Linda Humphries, Marc and Donna Wright, Janae Cormier, David Woolfe, Karen Ceaser, Mark Sturgis, Tonnie Emerson, Cheauvon Latrice Brown, Kathy Stefan, Eva Clark, David and Lin Wang, Pastors Brad and Carolyn Kuechler, Gabe Martinez, Maria Gabriel Arraige, Paul and Henrester Carter, Mark Gonzales, Vanessa Moore, and James Perry II.

Those who entrusted me with your stories for this book, thank you for sharing and having the heart of God to forgive so that others can be inspired to follow your journey of forgiveness.

Thank you all.

Introduction

Then Peter came to Jesus and asked, "Lord how many times shall I forgive my brother or sister who sins against me? Up to seven times?" Jesus answered, "I tell you, not seven times, but seventy-seven times"
                                                            (Matthew 18:21-22 NIV).

As the keynote speaker at a luncheon at St. Andrew United Methodist Church in Santa Maria, I shared my many traumatic experiences that caused unforgiveness—abandonment, childhood molestation, low self-esteem, bullying, racism, and domestic violence. I talked about my deep pain and my inability to relieve it. The turning point that released my shackles of unforgiveness was getting into God's Word about forgiveness and looking at various steps to forgiveness. Here, I was able to find resolve.

After the luncheon, I was approached by a woman who had been blinded by a doctor's negligence. "How can I forgive him?" she asked. "How do I move on with my life?"

I had been expecting her question and so I was prepared to answer. Several hours before the event, as I was praying for God's favor over my presentation, I was compelled by the

Holy Spirit with great fluidity: *"A woman who needs to know how to forgive will come to you after the luncheon and seek advice on forgiveness."* I never questioned the guidance of the Holy Spirit, although people frequently asked, "How do you know it is God speaking and not our inclinations?"

We find that before Jesus ascended to heaven, He informed His disciples that He would send a Helper, one who would teach, guide, and comfort those who believe in Him. "The Helper is the Holy Spirit. The Father will send Him in My place. He will teach you everything and help you remember everything I have told you" (John 14:26 NLV).

When you believe in Christ, the Holy Spirit immediately becomes a permanent part of your life. "For all who are led by the spirit of God are children of God" (Romans 8:14 NLT). Knowledge of God's Word can help us to tell whether or not our desires come from the Holy Spirit. We have to test our inclinations against Scripture—the Holy Spirit will not prod us to do anything contrary to God's Word. If it conflicts with the Bible, then it is not from the Holy Spirit and should not be embraced. As we meditate on Scriptures, study them, and read them, the Holy Spirit will speak to our hearts: "I am telling you these things now while I am still with you. But when the Father sends the Advocate as my representative—that is, the Holy Spirit—he will teach you everything and will remind you of everything I have told you" (John 14:25-26 NLT).

Furthermore, Jesus tells His followers that His sheep would know Him, and recognize His voice. "For sure, I tell you, the man who goes into the sheep-pen some other way than through the door is one who steals and robs. The shepherd of the sheep goes in through the door. The one who watches the door opens it for him. The sheep listen to the voice of the shepherd. He calls his own sheep by name and he leads them out. When the shepherd walks ahead of them, they follow him because they know his voice. They will not follow someone they do not know because they do not know his voice. They will run away from him" (John 10:1-5 NLV).

As a follower of Christ since the age of ten, I have known the Holy Spirit to speak to other Christians and me through dreams, visions, people, or a confirmation like what happened when that woman approached me.

After praying, I took a small Post-it and jotted down four tools for her to begin her forgiveness journey.

1. Be honest about what happened.
2. Be willing to let go of your unforgiveness baggage.
3. Take time to forgive yourself.
4. Embrace your re-birth.

At the event, many people came up to me with accolades. That one woman was *the only one* who sought help.

When she approached me, she had read my book, *Unmasking: A Woman's Journey*, and was moved by it. I remember hugging her through her brokenness. I listened intensely how her doctor had caused her blindness and that in a few days, she was going to see him. In a tone of bitterness she was prepared to tell him how he had destroyed her life.

I told her the Holy Spirit had spoken to my heart and I was expecting her. I proceeded to explain each tool in detail.

During the coming week, she continued to pray for better understanding on how to release the bitterness of unforgiveness toward her doctor before seeing him. Yes, she had to express her hurt, but she had to do it lovingly and in a context of forgiveness. Her visit ended well. She was able to forgive her physician for such an egregious act.

I have met hundreds of people who, like this woman, were encumbered with unforgiveness, and didn't know how to lift the heavy burden.

The message is simple, Forgiveness is a choice.

- "Put out of your life all these things: bad feelings about other people, anger, temper, loud talk, bad talk which hurts other people, and bad feelings which hurt other people. You must be kind to each other. Think of the other person. Forgive other people just as God forgave you because of Christ's death on the cross" (Ephesians 4:31-32 NLV).
- "If we confess our sins, He is faithful and just to forgive us our sins and to cleanse us from all unrighteousness" (I John 1:9 NKJV).
- "If you forgive others the wrongs they have done to you, your Father in heaven will also forgive you. But if you do not forgive others, then your Father will not forgive the wrongs you have done" (Matthew 6:14-15 GNT).

The stories may not be easy to read. The injury done in people's lives is profound, but the message is uplifting and true. We all have experienced pain and trauma. Moving forward is not the result of exacting revenge but of giving forgiveness.

I know this because of my own pain and suffering as a child that morphed into bigger challenges as an adult, leaving wounds open for forty years. It took me that long to empty my heart of the things that damaged me as a child and festered as an adult.

I pray the unforgiveness that you may have, whether inflicted on you or pain you caused others, will be released after reading the stories in this book, and that it not take you forty years. Trust me: that is much too long to be consumed by fear, conflict, hate, and anger.

Application and steps of forgiveness are important. You have the chance to get it out of your system, to understand what was done, and to avoid future error.

My parents were devout Christians and leaders in the Pentecostal movement. They meant well, did the best they could, but were extremely rigid. They would have us children settle fights by telling us not to argue. If we did, we would have to "kiss where we hit." That wasn't always fun. Sometimes, if we refused to cooperate, we would stand in a corner on one foot until we surrendered. Forgiveness itself felt like a punishment. Today, there are less punitive ways to teach kids to solve conflict.

There was no talk therapy, we just went on living as if nothing happened. Or, family would carry secrets to their grave.

There was no healing process. No steps given. I moved on with much of my childhood traumas, but the deep dark secret of molestation by a family member that occurred at age eight, played in my mind daily. I told no one. Then into my fifties, I entertained thoughts of ending my life.

This was a dear price having no healing therapy. Herein lies why it's essential to learn how to forgive as quickly as possible. Many of you may be like I was at one time. You find forgiving difficult. Think about the health consequences of holding onto unforgiveness. The medical and care giving communities classify unforgiveness as a disease and emotional disorder. Dr. Michael Barry, author and director of pastoral care, says it best. "Emotional stress, many times caused by unforgiveness, causes high levels of cortisol and adrenaline in the body, which cause wear and tear on the heart and cardiovascular system. And anger might not be the only culprit. High levels of anxiety and depression may contribute to health problems as well. Those who are angry much of the time tend to have other chronic negative emotions as well."[1] Dr. Barry further states that unforgiveness can be prevented, treated, and cured.

Once you begin the journey of forgiveness, you take on the heart of God: "Therefore, if anyone is in Christ, the new creation has come: The old has gone, the new is here!" (2 Corinthians 5:17 NIV).

DENISE
Forgiving Emotional Family Baggage

I was about four years old when my mom took my two younger sisters and me to Clarendon, Jamaica, to live with her dad and her stepmother. Mom took my two sisters to live with her in Kingston, Jamaica, leaving me in the country with my grandparents. This was from the early 1970s to 1987. I always thought she'd kept my sisters because they were younger and our dad had died.

I was wrong.

Life was hard in Clarendon. On the property were two houses made of concrete; one for my grandparents and a small two-room house made of bamboo and dirt. I shared a room with my older cousin, and my uncle stayed in the other room. We had an outside kitchen with a wooden fireplace and an outside toilet. Over time, they built a three-room house and my cousin and I moved into the one room. There was no running water or electricity. We had to walk a half mile to fetch drinking water or get to the main road. We washed our clothes and took our baths in the Rio Minho River.

My mom and sisters lived in a four-bedroom home with two baths, a living room, and a kitchen.

I came to understand that my mom didn't want me living with her because I was ugly and she was embarrassed by me. It made me very angry—but not at her, at *myself*. My mom was beautiful, petite with dark, smooth skin. If only I looked like her I would have been with her in the city.

Growing up in Jamaica, I wasn't allowed to question my mom or to express anger toward her. I had to keep everything inside. I remember going to spend time with her one summer, and she told me to call her by her first name instead of "Mommy."

When I was a little girl, going to Kingston was the highlight of my life. I was so happy just to be with my mom. And, being in Kingston meant running water and electricity. I could even watch television! I loved spending time with my sisters.

It wasn't until I was older and looked back at those days that I realized how, deep down in my heart, I was hurting.

I had my daughter when I was twenty-two years old. She was my second child with two different fathers. I'd had my first child at sixteen. It was my way of dealing with my hurt. I was looking for love and acceptance in the wrong places.

For years, I blamed my mom for my unhappiness. It was not until I gave my life to the Lord that I started to see things differently. In 1993 I attended a Friday night service while living in New York as a single mom of two. The message was *Unchain Me, Lord.*

I left the service without going to the altar, but the minister's words resonated in my heart all night. Early the next morning, I told the Lord, "I'm the same as that man that was chained up in the graveyard. Please unchain me and set me free." Saying those words began a two-sided love relationship between God and me. I was reminded of a person in the Bible by the name of Joseph. When his mother died, he was sold into slavery by his brothers.

Joseph had to go through many trials in Egypt, even being wrongfully accused and jailed. But through his trials, God used him, and he rose to the top of leadership. I strongly believed that God used me by putting me in every situation, ultimately delivering me from every hurt, disappointment, resentment, pain, and blame, and filled my heart with love.

My heart changed with this understanding. I came to realize that living with my grandparents in the country was the time of prosperity for me, as the seven years of prosperity were for Joseph. It was my grandmother who took me to church and introduced me to Jesus and the Word of God.

For many years, I was the only born-again person in my family. God told me when He saved me that He had my family in mind and my job was to intercede for them when I considered storing up supplies for the famine, just as Joseph had done when Pharaoh put him in charge.

When the bad days came to my family, the Holy Spirit would bring things to my mind, just as John 12:26 (NLT) wrote,

"Anyone who wants to serve me must follow me, because my servants must be where I am. And the Father will honor anyone who serves me." The Lord always gave me the words to encourage them. Now, I'm the person people in my family call to pray for this, and pray for that, and ask, "What do you think about this?"

Having Jesus in my life has kept me from being bitter toward my mom. She is now born-again and on fire for God. In 1987, we came to the United States and for the first time, I got to live with her full time. That was when she began to accept me.

My sisters would argue with her and disrespect her, but it was different with me. I gave her respect even when I disagreed with her. I have grown to love my mother with all my heart; she loves me and my children, and she tells us how much she loves us every chance she gets.

I found it so easy to forgive Mom after the Lord let me know it was not about my mom, but it was all about the plans He had for my life.

After moving to New York, I did not go to church for a long time, but the things that I learned in Jamaica came back to mind whenever I was going through hard times. My love and passion for the Lord is so great that I would not exchange those bad days. I'm able to use the things I lived to minister to others.

I could join Joseph when he said, "You intended to harm me, but God intended it all for good. He brought me to this position so I could save the lives of many people" Genesis 50:20 (NLT).

The "You" in this quote is not my mom; it's the devil, because I know I was not fighting flesh and blood. To God be the glory.

The Bible states that everything in our lives works toward our good. While we are in the situation it may not feel good, it hurts, but look toward the good that will come out of it. Genuine forgiveness is a greater help to you than the person you forgive.

I believe forgiveness is the tool that helps to take away the hurt and pain that is inflicted on you. When you forgive, you can remember the hurt and disappointment, but without the *pain* of it.

IRMA
Forgiving My Bully in an Unusual Way

I was twelve, a new immigrant from Mexico and struggling to fit in at a new elementary school—something *any* twelve-year-old girl would struggle with. That I was still learning English only made it harder. Still, while the language barrier made life more challenging, I was hardly shy. I was well-liked by my peers and I was a good student. I had every reason to be hopeful. Until, that is, I became the target of what we now call bullying.

Maybe my difficulty with English contributed. Maybe not. All I know is that one day, a girl named Diane cursed me out and I had no idea what she was saying. I knew it was bad, though. Her gestures and body language made that clear. That I didn't, or couldn't, respond to her seemed to only make her angrier. I stared at her, silently begging her for clarity but she took my stare as a challenge and set about wanting to fight me. She soon mobilized a group of friends—her "gang"—to make plans to jump me.

I had nightmares and woke up shaking and in tears. When I told my teacher about what was happening, she just told me that if anything happened to run to the principal's office. But that was only if they jumped me at school. What if they jumped me away from school?

A day came when it seemed the whole school knew I was going to be beaten up that afternoon—away from school. At lunch, I ran home and I told my aunt what was going on. She called the police. The officer walked me and my sister back to school and explained to the principal what seemed to be going on. The principal promised me that everything would be all right and he would take care of everything.

You can imagine how it looked to the rest of the school, having a police officer walk my sister and me into the principal's office. The rumor was that we'd been caught shoplifting at a local supermarket!

The bullying stopped at school, but Diane also lived nearby and kept harassing me outside school. Time, and new experiences, softens some of the rough edges. As the years went by, Diane stopped. This was the worst school experience I have ever had in my life. The only thing that turned the bullying around was that we eventually attended separate junior high and high schools. As years went by, her anger towards me diminished, but my own feelings of terror didn't diminish.

Once, I rented the movie, *Flatliners*. The story is about a group of friends who experiment with a near-death experience by stopping their hearts momentarily. In the movie, when a person dies, they revisit everyone they wronged and then they become a victim. The movie gave me a deep sense of satisfaction, knowing there was a possibility that Diane would suffer the same grief she inflicted on me.

* * *

I loved the manicurist I went to and, as sometimes happens when you spend time talking, we became friends. Even though she was a bit older, she seemed to be able to relate really well. I'd been going to have my nails done in her shop for several years. When I was there one day, suddenly, the door opened, and I froze. It was Diane.

She didn't even notice me. She walked right up to my friend.

"Mom..." she began and then had a brief conversation.

My heart was racing! I could hardly breathe. The conversation might have been ten seconds. It might have been ten minutes. I wouldn't have known. And, just as she walked in, she walked out.

"Are you okay?" my friend asked, feeling how my hands were shaking.

I nodded my head but the truth was I wasn't okay. It was ironic to say the least. Diane's mom and I had become good friends. Just as I had shared with her stories about my family, she had shared stories about hers. I now understood that the uncles she talked about being in gangs were Diane's uncles. That her daughter had become "hard" because of them.

My manicurist was sweet and kind. But now that Diane had reappeared in my life, every time I saw my manicurist, I felt the same dread I'd felt in school all those years earlier.

I finally told Diane's mom what her daughter had done to me. She laughed it off as something that happened "a long time ago." Maybe, I thought, it was a long time ago and I should let it go.

But I couldn't.

One afternoon, I stopped by the salon after work. It wasn't my regular day so she was surprised to see me, but I was more surprised by what she asked me. She asked if I could drive her to the hospital because her daughter's father had just passed away.

I felt a hollowness in the pit of my stomach. I remembered the grief Diane had caused me. Now, I had a choice to either respond as a Christian and friend or let my hurt fester into vengeance toward Diane.

It felt so easy to hold that bitterness in my heart. But it did not feel right. Instead, God opened my heart to take advantage of the opportunity to allow Diane and her mom to show me how to forgive. It was time to let my anger go.

I took my friend to the hospital.

I thought how sad it was that she had no one else to carry her. Then I realized that it wasn't sad but part of God's plan. It became a pivotal moment for God to show me how to forgive.

Today, I work with youth and many times use forgiveness as a lesson. I let them know the pain they carry is hurtful. Instead of carrying it, they need to shed it.

MARVIN
Finding Courage to Forgive Through My Adoption

How do you find your way back to someone who has turned her back on you?

However successfully adoptees go through life, they often grapple with the truth that their birth mother chose not to keep them, that the single person who is "supposed" to love them most of all turned away from them.

For Marvin, his decision to search for his birth mother had less to do with unresolved feelings than the fact that his son was born with a rare, and thankfully minor, hereditary birth defect. Understanding the power of heredity, his son—and his wife's encouragement—convinced him to consider searching for his biological mother.

The journey took twenty years. When it began, Marvin played a script in the back of his mind, one he imagined he would speak when he met his birth mother and, possibly, any birth siblings he might have.

Of course, as usually happens, life doesn't play out in the same way we imagine in the scripts we write for ourselves.

Marvin, once convinced to begin the search, began with some information his adoptive father gave him; that their family physician—who happened to be the first African American doctor in their community in the 1950s when he was born—had a hand in the adoption. He then spoke with social workers at the Michigan Department of Social Services adoption agency. It did not require much research on their part to discover Marvin's birth parents. However, they were not allowed to tell Marvin how to find them because his birth parents had not given permission for the agency to disclose the information.

Limited in what he was allowed to do, Marvin wrote letters that the social workers forwarded to his birth parents. Meanwhile, he was given some information about his birth family and his early years in an orphanage, but the information was carefully presented to have no identifying information.

After years of silence from his birth parents, Marvin received a letter from them along with a photograph of them.

Marvin was astonished how clearly he looked like his birth parents, particularly his father. Marvin exclaimed, "Imagine having gone through life looking at every stranger you encountered and wondering, 'Is it you?'... to finally see them!"

The letter they sent told him a little bit about his birth family's history.

With a photograph and a little information, the search became a family affair. Marvin's children took to the internet to further the search. There were highs and lows, hopeful moments and dead ends. When Marvin received an anonymous phone call telling him that his birth father had passed away, he was convinced that the search was over. Ironically, his birth father's death opened a door to more information. His oldest son, then a funeral director, was able to learn more about Marvin's birth family. And then his daughter, bold and adventurous as only someone who grew up on the internet could be, used Facebook to reach out to one of the granddaughters mentioned in his birth father's obituary.

That allowed for the first actual contact between Marvin's family and his birth family. His daughter visited the West Coast where the granddaughter lived. Her visit led to the beginning of a relationship with Marvin's birth family the following year.

However, it would be another six years before he would meet his birth mother.

He was filled with trepidation before the meeting. His birth mother had been in declining mental health. The beginnings of her dementia were obvious to Marvin. However, she was lucid in her conversation with him. When he sat next to her, she took his hands and looked into his eyes. It was the summer of 2015.

"I knew this day would come," she told him.

She told him how happy she had been when she got his letter all those years earlier and learned that his adoptive family had been good to him. She also expressed that his late birth father loved him as well. "I love you, and Sam loved you too."

Still, she was clearly upset during the visit. She asked him a number of times to please forgive her for not being in his life.

"Of course I forgive you," he told her.

As soon as he said those words, he could sense that she felt released from any guilt and shame she'd felt for giving him up for adoption over sixty years earlier. His forgiveness released her from the weight she'd carried all those years, a weight imposed on her by a culture and system that insisted that unmarried girls give up their babies for adoption.

Years and years of guilt and uncertainty, sorrow and loss—on both of their parts—were released by Marvin's ability to forgive.

"I believe my birth mother and I made peace with the past," Marvin said.

His actual meeting with his birth mother far exceeded the script he'd written in his imagination all those years earlier, for his script never anticipated the power and grace of that forgiveness.[2]

4

MARGARET
Forgiving My Mother for the Abuse

It is not easy to find a way to forgive when the one you have to forgive is the one who gave you life. We like to think that mothers welcome their children into the world and that they will love and nurture them. That was not my experience. Usually, when a mother doesn't really want a child it's because she isn't ready for a child or another child. But that wasn't the case for me. My mother loved my younger brother. No, my mother never wanted *me*.

She said she didn't even know she was pregnant with me. She went to the doctor, not feeling good, and they admitted her to the hospital—two weeks before my birth. She cried and cried. She took my name from some book they gave her.

I was already disruptive when I entered kindergarten. My behavior got me a beating after the first parent-teacher conference. Soon enough though, I grew overly quiet and withdrawn. I got bullied. I felt that nobody cared about me. They called me "fat," "ugly," "stupid," "lazy," and "worthless," and you can bet I felt all of those things. Through the years, I learned not to go to her for anything. I was on my own to figure things out. I gave up and ran away from home when I was fourteen.

At seventeen, I got married for a short time. It seemed like an escape. When it ended, I became promiscuous. I smoked a lot of weed. I was troubled. And I wondered why nobody loved me.

In my twenties, the turmoil of my life kept going. The difference was that now I could lash back and go home. There were times when the fights were my fault. I was filled with bitterness and I wanted payback.

Still, my eyes saw things differently. I was growing up and I could start to appreciate her as a person. She'd had a hard life. My father was a violent alcoholic who beat her. She divorced him when I was nine, but the die was cast. She went about choosing the same kind of men. So she had her own issues. Sure, she was wrong to take it out on me but people got to do the best they can. In my thirties, I decided to try to get past all the madness. I think, in her own way, she wanted to make up too. I found it very hard to receive affection from her, but she said she loved me. She always helped me and was nothing but a loving grandma to my children. I realized I couldn't undo the wrongs done me. But I could work past them. I decided to just start with the little things. Visiting her, calling her, offering her help as she got old. I didn't want her to die with all that between us.

Most importantly, I had to forgive her for *my sake*. Of course, I still remember things, but *I didn't want to carry that weight anymore*. We have a choice, I think, you start with the decision and work it out from there. Whatever the circumstances, we have that choice to move forward and get unstuck.

I went to visit my mother one morning not knowing a neighbor had found her dead sometime earlier. Her body was still there. My brother met me at the elevator. We waited for the mortuary and I sat with her—in peace.

* * *

I am short with a small frame, like our father and his family. With puberty, I got chubby. She ragged me about my weight, being a big woman herself. She would say that my sister was size four so why wasn't I size four?

Fat, ugly, and stupid.

My younger brother was sweet and sensitive. We'd fight sometimes but were close. We were alone a lot. My mother had to work so we let ourselves in after school. During the summer, we were each other's company. We depended on each other. After my mom divorced my dad, she started taking diet pills and lost over a hundred pounds. She dyed her hair, wore make up, and bought new clothes. In short, she blossomed. She went out a lot, either on dates or with her friends. She was in her mid-thirties to mid-forties.

Physical punishment was my mother's parenting "go to." I was slapped, punched with a fist, and beaten. As bad as that was, the emotional abuse was worse. She was obsessed with cleanliness. I had to come from school and clean house every day. When she came home, it was inspection time. And of course, I "could never do anything right." The house could be spotless, and I was still "good for nothing" or "worthless."

As I got older, I grew quiet and withdrawn. I was bullied in school which, according to my mother, was what I deserved. She told me that she wouldn't want to be friends with me either. Or that she wouldn't sit with me at school.

Emotionally, I was just beat up by a young age. If I had a voice, I'd lost it and didn't find it until adulthood.

I ran away at fourteen to San Francisco. I jumped on a Greyhound bus and got as far as Bakersfield before the driver discovered me. He threw me off the bus, so I hitchhiked the rest of the way. It was 1969, and whatever magic there had been during the "Summer of Love" was gone. The city was full of runaways like me, lost children. We found common ground and became friends. We helped and looked out for each other. We survived by panhandling and shoplifting.

Ironically, my upbringing helped me survive. Growing up with my mother made me wary and untrusting—the perfect personality for life on the streets. Growing up in chaos, I wasn't easily rattled. Even though I had bravado, I was still just a kid and there was real danger on those streets, with bad people looking to prey on vulnerable street kids. Talk of love and peace was just another way to take advantage. Addicts, hustlers, and pimps roamed those streets. After three months, I just walked up to a police car and turned myself in.

I'm not proud of what I did. Back then, I felt very uncared about, but now I know what my family went through. My brother went AWOL from the army to come home after I left. My mother put my picture in the newspaper, certain I'd been kidnapped. My younger brother told me he'd never forgive me for what I put her through.

When I got home, she wasn't relieved. She was angry. She was sure I'd just wanted to have an adventure. I was a bad girl and she made sure I knew it. She said all the kids at school would know it too, and they would be even meaner to me.

But that's not what happened. I was welcomed back to school with hugs and lots of questions. Turns out, I'd been the talk of the school and a lot of the kids were curious about what I'd done and where I'd gone. But I was bored by that "adventure." I just wanted to move forward.

Of course, I was interested in boys. Mother was clear that they were only interested in one thing. "They probably think you're *easy* because you've run away," she sneered at me.

I had my first boyfriend at fifteen. My first kiss. Despite what my mother said, it was innocent and nice. He was a good guy.

Shortly before my sixteenth birthday, Mom introduced me to a young man who was nearly twenty, the brother of one of her close friends. After he'd come around a couple of times, she said that he liked me. I wasn't attracted to him at all, but soon, he was coming to dinner and tagging along if we went somewhere. Unlike her attitude with other boys, she let me go places with him: to dinner, the mall, the movies. I was happy to get out of the house. I warmed up to him but I didn't like him like I liked some of the boys at school. But as you can imagine, going out led to one thing or another, and he started wanting sex. After resisting, I finally consented because my sixteen-year-old hormones were in the driver's seat. It was not a good experience.

But having had sex once, now he expected it. He told me he'd marry me. I told my mother—not everything, just that he wanted to marry me. I didn't know what to do. She wasn't much help. She went to him and asked why would he want to marry ME?

She said we had to wait at least a year, until I was seventeen. I was just on this track, going forward. Things continued as they were. We fought but he was also getting something out of it. We had nothing in common. I tried to break up with him, but Mom was always in the middle. He was a manipulator. He said my mother would believe him before me and threatened to tell her about the sex. He saw the relationship my mother and I had. He'd go to her and she'd come after me. It was crazy. He was her friend's brother, but she and her friend stopped talking. Maybe it had something to do with it.

Then, I had a pregnancy scare. That was crazy. My mother cried and went on about how I had betrayed her trust in me. Notice, this was now about *her*. She was always the victim. When I finally said, "What about me?" her answer was, "You should have thought of that before you opened your legs." I was a bad girl again and ruined my life. I wasn't pregnant but she said if I was going to do it, I might as well be married.

I saw a logic in that too. I could get away from my mother. It was a way out. For me, marriage was freedom. She maintained that she was begging me not to do it, that I was "so in love." That wasn't true. I thought about telling her I didn't want to go through with it, but she put her heart into giving me a wedding. She was spending money; my sister and brother had previously married at city hall. I felt bad. He spent money too, but I guess I didn't want to disappoint HER. When I got my wedding pictures, I left them in the envelope in a drawer. I was surprised she bought an album for her copies.

My thought was, I can always get a divorce.

When I got pregnant, I was happy. I wanted a baby. No matter what I thought of his father, I loved that baby. I felt nothing but love for him from the day he was born. When the baby was seven months old, I told my husband I was leaving. He said I wasn't, but it was his pride, not his heart talking. By that time we hardly spoke to each other. He was taking longer and longer to come home. I had no desire to do anything for him.

I waited until he fell asleep and drove to my nearby sister's. In the morning, he came for the car but didn't ask about me. Instead, he went to my mother who stormed right over and ordered me back.

"No."

She smacked me hard, so my sister had to step in. Mom was so angry she didn't speak to me for six months. Once, I was pushing my son in the stroller and she drove right past me.

In time, my husband had lost contact completely. I filed for divorce and found myself on welfare. I was nineteen, but I was free. I reconciled a bit with my mom but she still tried to control me. She refused to babysit if I wanted to go somewhere and have fun. She told me that my youth was "lost."

I just stopped asking her. Things were hard sometimes, but I never felt my life was over. I never felt trapped. Looking back, I think that's how Mom felt about *her* life and so, she was putting that on me.

Turns out, whatever else I can say bad about my mom, she was a very good grandma. My son was her fifth grandchild. When she watched him, she took very good care of him. When he was school age, she took him to and from school because by then I was working full time. She gave him a birthday party in her yard, something we'd never had. She bought him his school clothes every year. It seemed as she got older, she calmed down. She learned a lot from her own hardships.

She fought a lot with my oldest brother. He was close to my dad and very much like him. He had my dad's sense of humor and charm, but he also became an alcoholic just like Dad. And just like in Dad, alcohol brought out the worst in him.

He knew it all firsthand. He had to protect my mom many times. But that didn't seem to keep him away from drinking. After my parents divorced, he was drafted and went to Vietnam. When he came home on leave, he always talked about what he went through. It was like he was trying to purge himself. I was still a kid. I'd hear him having nightmares and it scared me. But he liked army life and decided to make it his career.

That also meant a second tour in Vietnam.

The war ended, he stayed in the army, and he still drank. In 1976 he was stationed in Texas. He had orders for Germany and came home before he had to leave. The whole family was at Mom's house and there was beer. He got drunk and started a fight with her boyfriend, which led to a shouting match with our mother. He left, but he was a mean drunk and Mom was very upset and crying.

He knew he'd gone too far and called the next day to apologize, but she wouldn't talk to him. He tried again, she refused. He went back to Texas and called. She didn't want to talk to him. He told my sister he started going to AA meetings. One night my younger brother answered the phone; Mom wasn't home. He said to tell Mom he'd call later. He asked him to convince her to talk to him.

But he didn't call. Instead, hours later, the army hospital called to say he'd been hit by a drunk driver and was in ICU. He had both legs and his pelvis broken as well as massive internal injuries. He'd been bleeding out when the ambulance got there.

Mom, my sister, and my middle brother were on a plane the next day. Mom slept at the hospital when she could sleep. My brother was conscious but didn't speak because he couldn't breathe on his own. Mom never left his side. She held his hand. She told him she was going to take him home and take care of him. He hung on for a week, but he died of his injuries at just thirty years of age.

It was devastating. At the funeral, I was next to her waiting to enter the church. She said, "Don't leave me. Stay with me." So, I put my arm around her and supported her as we walked behind the casket.

It was easily two years before she was herself again. Right after the funeral, she bought a plot so she could be buried near him. She was at the cemetery daily. She said she couldn't stay away. She didn't sleep. She said she saw him every time she closed her eyes. She went from this strong, imposing figure to crying and just broken. She said she never thought about losing one of her children.

It was then she told me she loved me.

I didn't know how to receive that. I'd never heard it before. It made me uncomfortable to be hugged. It just felt so... so strange. I wasn't used to it. I'm still not used to it. I like my space.

Time helped; she smiled again and started to go places and do things.

We still had our moments, but she never went without speaking to me again. If I left angry, she came to make sure I got home safely. I still had a lot of resentment in my early twenties. I'd say things that I knew were hurtful to her. I wanted to pay her back for how much she'd hurt me. And sometimes she was her old self.

I started seeing a wonderful therapist. I realized that if my mom was sorry, she could never admit it because it would mean she did wrong. Her whole persona was this good, kind-hearted person who helped people. She couldn't say she was sorry, but she showed it by going out of her way for me. She bought all my son's school clothes and took care of him so I could work. She helped me buy a car. She bought me clothes for my first office job. And I could see some of the things I said really were hurtful. So, I decided to work harder at resolving the past. It couldn't be undone. It wasn't doing me any good to keep returning to it.

As I got older and was able to see her as a whole person, I could appreciate what she had gone through. She had a lot of pain and hardship in her own life. She'd lost her father, whom she loved, while still a child. My grandmother, by this time with six children, had an affair. My grandfather told her to give the other man up, but she refused. So, he left his whole family. My grandmother's last four children were fathered by this other man who also left her. Sometimes Mom would tell us about her father and cherished her only picture of him.

Maybe that was why she always had to have a man in her life. She didn't learn to be alone until well into her senior years. When I was younger, I resented it, but later I could laugh that at her age she always had someone to take her to dinner and a movie.

In some ways, she was ahead of her time. She always worked outside the home. When she got tired of her low-paying, dead-end job, she learned new skills and found factory work. I could see her owning her own business if she was doing that today. She had the head and the financial sense to do it. She was a talented decorator. Our home was immaculate; she bought the best she could afford. She had an eye for color, space, and putting things together.

So, what did I learn from her?

Manners are important. Don't interrupt. Keep yourself groomed and as well-dressed as you can afford. Have some money saved. Don't accept things at face value, look at all the angles and size up situations and people. Nobody gives you something for nothing. Don't believe everything you hear. Ask questions. Never sign something without reading it. I still learned all the life skills from her. When I became a Christian, the church helped me learn about forgiveness by studying the Word of God and the teachings of how Christ forgave.

So, there it is.

This is our story, my mother and me. We came down a long, hard road together. I find that I am my mother's daughter. Sometimes I catch myself being like her in some way. I look the most like her too, so there's the mirror. Forgiveness is hard, but it's not always for the other person. It's for you, so you can move on, have some peace, and strive not to make the same mistakes. You can choose. So, for your own sake, choose well.

5

VANESSA
Healing Childhood Memories "Too Ugly, Too Dark"

It has taken me more than forty years to be able to say—and mean—"I am Black and beautiful."

Not long ago, a friend told me that I was beautiful and, as I always did, I stared at him and said, "Yeah, right."

He was amazed. "You don't see the beauty in yourself?"

I shook my head. All I saw was black and ugly. In other words, I say what I was always told to see.

I had lived my entire life believing that my dark, black skin was a curse. Being "cursed," I never let anyone get too close. After all, I believed I didn't deserve to be loved.

"Until you can look in the mirror and love the person who is looking back at you, you will never see yourself as beautiful," he said softly. "You will never be happy, and neither will anyone around you."

Those words resonated in my soul and changed my life. For the first time, I began to look at myself and to actually like the person looking back at me. It took some time, but I did begin to realize that I am beautiful. Not only that, but my dark, black skin was *the reason* I was so beautiful, not a curse!

* * *

I am a "middle child," number four of seven, born January 1961. Of all of us, I am the one with the darkest skin.

I remember one day—gosh, it still cuts me so to recall it!— I could not have been more than twelve years old. I heard my mother speaking on the telephone. Just as I was passing through from my bedroom through the kitchen, I heard her say just as matter-of-fact as if she was talking about the weather, "I should have aborted my fourth child when I had the chance..."

I stopped dead in my tracks. The math was simple. *I* was her fourth child. Hot tears began to run down my cheeks. My throat began to tighten. I started to shake. Just then, she looked up and saw me. Her eyes widened and she dropped the phone. She reached out to hold me but her hug felt stiff. She didn't apologize for *what* she said, just that I'd overheard her say it. "I never meant for you to know that."

* * *

All of my life I was told that I was too black and too ugly to amount to anything. No one would ever give an ugly, Black girl a chance.

All my life I was told this by my mother.

I was the child she *shouldn't* have had, born of a man she was not married to, a man she loved but could not have. So I was a constant, painful reminder to her that she would never be with the man she loved. In addition, my birth shamed her husband and his family.

When I was small, I did not know this. I just knew that I was not loved like my siblings. I did everything I could to try to make her happy. I was a straight-A student, graduating at the top of my high school class. I was offered scholarships to eight different colleges.

Was she proud? Was she happy? No, instead she cursed me for wanting to go to college. She wanted me to turn them all down. But I left and went to the one furthest away. I promised myself I would not become what she said I would, a failure.

The only one who cared was my grandmother. No matter what my mother said or did, she would say, "You got to forgive her and never stop loving her." She told me to always follow my heart and that I would be able to do anything I desired.

So when she called me at two a.m. with news that something was wrong, I knew I had to respond. She said my mother was sick. Very sick. Her words hit me hard. Even though she was hardly the loving, nurturing, and supportive mother I wanted or that other people had, I tried to always love her because she was my mother.

She had suffered a heart attack and now her heart was enlarged and weak. Her blood pressure was sky high and she had a number of other ailments. I put aside how she'd treated me. I felt I had to make sure she was taken care of. After all, she was the only mom I had and no matter how she made me feel, I would always love her.

My sisters and brothers were all too busy with their own lives to make any sacrifice, so the burden fell to me. Deep inside, I knew that if anything happened to her and I didn't take the time to help or be there for her, I would regret it for the rest of my life.

I spent the next six weeks caring for her, night and day, losing thirty-five pounds in the process. A week before it was time to get back to my life, we went to my grandparents' house. The day after we arrived, my mom had a heart attack that kept her in the hospital for several weeks.

She could not go home again so, with my aunt and uncle's help, I arranged for her to move to live with my grandmother. I went to the hospital to say goodbye and to let her know what I had done on her behalf.

Was she grateful?

No, she cursed me. She told me she hated me and that she never wanted to see me again.

My grandmother had tried to console me. She told me I had done the right thing and that my mom would someday realize it. But in my heart, I felt I had failed her once again, no different than when I went to college without her blessings.

She had awakened me one morning a few weeks before I was scheduled to leave and told me to get all of my stuff and put it in the car. We drove eight hours to my new college.

"Get out," she said.

I got out and took my stuff out of the car. Then she drove off. I stood in front of my new school, with nowhere to sleep, no food or cash. All I could think was, *Why me? Am I that bad of a person that I should be treated this way?* As I stood there crying my eyes out, a teacher from summer school asked me what was happening. When I explained my situation, she told me it would be all right. I was given a room and a food card until the start of school. I didn't hear from my mom for over a month. She hadn't given any thought to what happened to me.

* * *

The last time I saw her was many years later. I asked her why she had treated me the way she did. She said, "I knew you could handle it."

That was her explanation.

I was overseas when I learned that she had passed. I felt as if someone had stuck a knife in my heart. I sat on the floor in a corner of my home, crying my eyes out. I thought of all the times that I had felt this same pain. I wasn't in agony because she had died. I was in agony because of words that were spoken or things that were done to me by my mother. The only difference this time was that I knew that I would never feel this pain again.

She was gone. I thought her words had been silenced, but I kept hearing them in my head and my heart.

It took me a long time to make peace within myself. I wondered if I had made all of my life's choices because of her or in spite of her. I look at my own children and who they have become, amazing young men who are focused and who have a determination of reaching goals that they set. Full of love from a mother who chose to love them with all of her heart and encouraged them to be anything their hearts desired, and who always made sure that they knew that they were the most important thing in her life.

When I look at them, I know that no matter what I had gone through in my life with my mom, that I had done something great with them. Every time I get a phone call from them or have the good fortune to spend some time with them, I get peace in knowing that God has helped me to know what not to do and how to show love to them, my children.

I still think of her from time to time, but not with fond memories.

God had showed me how to free myself by being unlike her, by doing the opposite with my children. He has helped me to realize that no matter how I got to where I am, everything that I have gone through in my life has made me the beautiful, smart, loving, and creative person I am today.

I had to let the hurt go so that I could give my two sons all the love that I have inside of me. I love them better than I had been loved. I encourage them through their good and their bad and I give them big hugs to let them know that they are amazing young men and that their mom loves them.

It's 2019. I now have an amazing life. I have been through many ups and downs, but I thank God that I made it through.

There are times, sometimes late at night, when I can still hear her voice telling me, "I knew you could handle it."

It is only now that I truly believe that I CAN.

GLORIA
Forgiving Racism Isn't Easy

December 1, 2015.

Noon.

At fifty-five degrees, the air in the affluent neighborhood of Rolling Hills Estates, California, had a bite to it. Retired for several years, I had decided to earn some extra Christmas money while doing a good deed by being a Salvation Army bell ringer in a local shopping center.

My friend Gary had just pulled up on his motorcycle to meet me for my thirty-minute lunch break. Just as I went to park the bell stand, a late-model SUV eased by. Inside, three young men, about high school age, were laughing loudly. They seemed to be no different than any of the other high school students who came to the shopping center. Affluent. Indifferent. Self-absorbed. I didn't give them much mind until the driver leaned across to the passenger's open window.

"Hey Black (expletive)! Wouldn't want to be a Nigger!"

My breath was taken from me. Had I really heard that? Had they...had he really said such a thing? To me? They continued laughing riotously, as if nothing funnier in the world had ever happened. The SUV eased into a nearby parking spot and the boys, all White, all laughing, got out of the vehicle and started walking toward me.

I felt frozen in place. What malice could they hold for me? What additional insult or harm did they want to inflict on me? They continued toward me. Just then, Gary slid his motorcycle helmet off. The boys slowed and looked at him, an African American man in black leather, and doubt flickered across their faces. Their direction changed and they went into a nearby store.

"Did I hear them right?" I asked, my voice shaky.

He nodded, his eyes still looking in the direction they'd gone.

As much as they were unnerved by Gary's presence, I was emboldened. I managed to capture a photo of them on my phone. I also took a picture of the vehicle and license plate number.

I am an older African American woman. I am retired from a rich and fulfilling professional life. I have friends and am well-respected. Yet the casual cruelty of these high school boys had gutted me. I felt degraded. I felt unsafe. I also felt angry. I was determined not to let the incident be forgotten.

I reported the incident to security at the shopping center. The security guard I spoke with, a thoughtful Latino, was not surprised by what had happened. He said many of the well-off

White kids from the area came to the shopping mall with a sense of entitlement. He himself had been heckled and verbally abused by them.

"They like to tell me that they get more in allowance than I make in salary," he said, shaking his head sadly.

As we spoke, he asked for a description of the boys. When I described them, particularly the driver, he nodded his head. He knew the boys. He said they were students at Palos Verdes Peninsula High School. "Jocks," he added, his voice making his feelings clear.

The young man had had an incident with another guard. He called the guard the "N-word" when he'd told him not to ride his skateboard on the sidewalk of the shopping center. The boy told him he didn't have to listen, seeing as his dad was "the richest man in town." The more I heard, the angrier I became—and the more determined to do something.

The next day, I filed an incident report with the Los Angeles County Sheriff's Department, Lomita Station. But even that experience seemed to heighten my sensitivity to the racial disparity in the area. I waited over forty minutes, during which time others were assisted. Finally, an African American deputy sheriff was exiting the lobby and asked if I had been helped. I shook my head and let him know what I had seen as I waited.

He went back into the office. When he came out, he told me someone would be with me as soon as possible. A very short time later, I was helped by a deputy sheriff. He took my statement, along with a picture of the car and license plate. He listened sympathetically. Then he told me it would be classified as a "hate incident" and not a "hate crime."

With a report number in hand, my demeaning, degrading, and disturbing experience was in the bureaucracy. Like every bureaucracy, it moved slowly and required constant prodding. I was happy to keep prodding. I made sure the sheriff's office knew that the NAACP was also interested in the case.

Subsequently, the detective assigned to the case reminded me that, "We are dealing with an incident here, not a crime." Further, he had limited authority to pursue the case as the individual was a student and he had been exercising his First Amendment right. He did say that he'd located the student based on the license plate number and had spoken with him at his home. The suspect admitted to what he'd said and done. He said he wanted to speak with me, but the detective told him no because I was angry.

I was astonished by this. I had every right to be angry but essentially to be dismissed as an "angry Black woman" was condescending and aggravating. It only added to the insult I'd felt from the incident. I was shaken and scared and angry about racism being alive and so close in 2015. I am a Black woman who had visions of being torched by the boys in the truck.

My experience was categorized as a hate incident. It could easily have been categorized as racial bullying, affluenza, and elder abuse. By whatever name it was called, it was harmful and destructive. My peace was compromised. It recalled youthful encounters in the South with the KKK. It recalled my elementary school teacher in Michigan who wouldn't touch us Black kids.

I found myself looking over my shoulder, ever fearful. I had trouble sleeping. My life was disrupted by this experience and I just couldn't allow that to go on.

I'd lived too long and learned too much. I had to do something. I refused to allow myself to be a "victim." I had to find a way to turn this into a positive.

But, before thinking about positives, I had to come to terms with my own complex feelings. Part of me wanted a protest against the school, the family, the culture that allowed this hate to fester and grow. I wanted to get back at all White folks who were racist. But conversations with my family and NAACP leaders convinced me that a protest would not change anything. Revenge or restitution could not be the goal. In prayer, I realized I had to become a beacon of hope to racial conflict.

Using contacts in the community, I arranged to meet with the principal, assistant principal, and campus security personnel. I was with a small group from the NAACP.

After reviewing the incident, the principal was neither in denial or defensive. She knew only too well that her students were entitled enough to behave thoughtlessly hateful. She was disappointed that it was the student it turned out to be; a student she'd worked with often, and had personally intervened to keep him from being suspended. "David," she sighed sadly. "How could it be David?"

David had been adopted. There was a chance he'd experienced neglect before he was adopted.

Just seventeen, he was soon to be eighteen and would be able to decide without his parents how he wanted to handle the situation.

"Let me speak with him," the principal said, after speaking with the superintendent and Board of Education. "If he chooses, maybe you can meet with him."

David did choose to meet with me and the delegation from the NAACP. And so it was, two months after that ugly December day, I came face to face with him. This young man who had so unnerved me and had damaged the safety I'd come to feel in my life. When David arrived, he could not have been more polite, greeting each of us with a handshake. Because I was not the only African American in the principal's office, I spoke up.

"David, I'm Gloria. From the shopping center."

He nodded in my direction.

I thanked him for admitting what he had done and being courageous enough to meet. "You know, you and I have a lot in common."

He blinked, looking a bit surprised both by the statement and the fact my tone was anything but hostile.

"We do?"

I told him I had once run track. "I had even aspired to go to the Olympics when I was in college. I never made it but later became one of the first African Americans to reach the summit of Mt. Kilimanjaro."

He seemed genuinely impressed.

"Let me know when your next meet is. I'd love to be there and support you."

He nodded. "Sure," he said. "That'd be great."

Having established a positive tone, I turned my attention to the incident. I was clear about my feelings as I expressed disappointment in him and his friends. "I have to ask, why did you do it?"

He shrugged. "I was showing off."

"Do you have any Black friends?" I asked him.

He shook his head. "I know Blacks at this school, but no Black friends."

Before the meeting ended, he was given an assignment to read my book and report on it. He had to commit to attending a Black history celebration in June. Since, it turned out, he was skilled in photography, a representative from the NAACP offered to have him be an official photographer at the event, with pay.

We then scheduled a follow-up meeting. By the time of that meeting, he had turned eighteen. An adult, he was now responsible for his decisions. I was disappointed that when I asked about my book he admitted he hadn't read it. He said he hadn't had time, between his new girlfriend, homework, and fulfilling assignments so he could graduate in June.

I was annoyed but I was not interested in having my annoyance derail whatever progress we had made and could still make.

I told him I was excited about coming to his track meet in a few weeks and of seeing him as the official photographer for the June event.

True to my word, I attended David's track meet. I cheered him on as he crossed the finish of the 800 meters in fourth place.

* * *

I still wrestle with whether I handled the situation in the best possible way. I have to believe I did as well as could be done. Like any Christian, we have a duty to seek peace with humankind, and forgive those who have wronged us.

When it comes to the sin of racism, we must seek God's Word to change our attitude and seek peace as Christ would do if He were on earth. I believe Christ would first acknowledge that racism is America's "original sin." To heal and be forgiven, we must follow some very determined steps as a nation.

1. We must recognize that America has a problem with race relations. Dr. Martin Luther King Jr. said it best, *"The thing wrong with America is white racism...However difficult it is to hear, however shocking it is to hear, we've got to face the fact that America is a racist country."*[3]

2. Seek face-to-face dialogue with others, specifically Whites and Blacks. America's history of slavery, civil rights battles, and current racial issues in America demands that we talk to one another. We will never deal effectively with race in America if we can't have a discussion about it. I've heard Whites say they didn't personally cause pre-and post-slavery racism, therefore they are not a part of the problem. They may not have perpetuated racism, but it's still with us, and they are in America, therefore they are

part of the solution. The question should become: *What can I do?*

3. Churches must take the lead in these discussions. We have been silent too long, afraid to take the moral position that racism is wrong. We must be about our Father's business. Matthew 5:14-16 NLT reminds us, "You are the light of the world—like a city on a hilltop that cannot be hidden. No one lights a lamp and then puts it under a basket. Instead, a lamp is placed on a stand, where it gives light to everyone in the house. In the same way, let your good deeds shine out for all to see, so that everyone will praise your heavenly Father."

One strategy that I applaud is feet washing among races. When I was growing up in the 1950s in a blue-collar neighborhood in Lansing, Michigan, our small Pentecostal Church would wash feet monthly of every member, Blacks, Whites, Latinos, and Indigenous Peoples. The act is decidedly humbling and a way to bring those who practice the heart of God together. It was also an act of cleansing and reconciliation.

Feet washing during biblical times was prevalent as a cultural custom and to show humility and hospitality. It was a practice Jesus did, girding himself with a towel and washing his disciples' feet. He said to them, "Now that I, your Lord and Teacher, have washed your feet, you also should wash one another's feet. I have set you an example that you should do as I have done for you" (John 13:14-15

NIV). We find that Abraham and others in the Old Testament admonished feet washing.

In America, the very idea of "sharing" water between the races has been anathema. Like public fountains, public transportation, and public schools, the public pool is often a battleground of racial segregation. Under Jim Crow era policy, not only could Black and Whites not swim at the same time, many pools were entirely off limits to Blacks, fueled by a fear that African Americans carried disease. Like the lunch counter and public buses, swimming pools became a point of protest. Foot washing is a powerful symbol that those days are behind us!

4. Schools have a responsibility to teach racial understanding in sessions like a "Day of Dialogue" or develop a curriculum where students are taught racial diversity.

5. Early intervention with continuous dialogue, never ending with all of society, the faith community, organizations, businesses, and neighborhoods. Open our doors and begin a discussion to tear down the walls of racism.

No one is born to hate. We are taught to hate. In the same way, we can be taught to love. We can be taught to be accepting and understanding.

We can be taught that everyone is worthy of dignity and respect.

7

JEREMIAH
Facing My Past and Embracing the Journey to Forgive

As an active duty officer in the United States Army, I had a traumatic experience that changed the course of my life forever. At the time, I could not know that I would have to make the hardest decision in my life and forgive my wife.

In 1999, I enlisted in the military. After three years of exceptional service, I was recommended by my commanding officer to enter an Officer Training Program. At that time, I was released from active duty and dual-enrolled in college and the Reserve Officer Training Corp. During my last year of college, I met my wife, got married, and had a child.

2001 was a momentous year. I was twenty-three years old. Within a year I became a husband, a father, and an officer. I graduated from college, received my commission into the Medical Service Corp, and was shipped off to Fort Hood, Texas. It was also the year the World Trade Center was brought down.

I quickly settled in my house and in my unit. I was excited for my wife and kids to join me. However, no sooner had they arrived, than the world I was accustomed to was turned upside down. In the past, my wife and I had gotten along beautifully— with only the everyday issues one always encounters in any relationship. But now, our problems seemed deep and intractable. We argued more often than we got along. The result of the increased tension in our home had me out most nights, drinking and doing drugs. My life began to spiral as I was spending too much time out partying with my enlisted soldiers. Not only was my home life falling apart, but I was violating many army rules and regulations. Worse still, I was violating my own personal values.

One night, after a long day of partying, my wife called my commander and reported what had been going on. She told him about my drug use, my behavior with my soldiers; the difficulties of our life. While military life is always challenging, I was clearly exhibiting conduct unbecoming of an officer.

My commanding officer had no choice but to call me in. The next day, I was summoned to be questioned and to undergo a drug test. The result was a foregone conclusion. My urinalysis came back positive for drug use.

With no reasonable doubt as to my behavior, I was removed from my position as the battalion medical officer, court-martialed, and charged with illegal drug use, fraternization, fraud, and a long list of other infractions. I plead guilty, served ten months in military confinement at Ft. Knox, and was released from the army with an Other Than Honorable discharge (OTH).

During my confinement, I stewed in my anger and resentment. When I was released, I continued to blame my wife for everything that had happened. I made no attempt to reconcile our marriage.

In 2007, my wife made the decision to get on with her life in a healthy way. She filed for divorce, married an ex-Marine, and moved to South Carolina to start a new life.

My own decision was to continue to let my resentment define my life. As a result, I continued to make unhealthy choices and, once again, my life spiraled out of control. Despite being an intelligent person, it took a lot of trial and error, a lot of looking directly at where my resentment had gotten me that I realized in order to move forward in life spiritually, emotionally, and financially, I needed to start by forgiving my ex-wife.

It was not easy but with the help of God, studying the Word, and the counsel of mentors, I was able to forgive my ex-wife. Today my ex-wife and I have a healthier relationship. We are able to cooperate with each other in order to parent the children we have together.

8

MEG
My Father's Infidelity, the Need to Forgive

"Give him a hug and say you're sorry."

This is the advice my mother gave me as a young girl when I'd fight with my siblings. Simple enough. I hit him. I took his toy. I hurt his feelings. Whatever I did, I apologized and my brother forgave me. If he hit me, or took my toy, or hurt my feelings, the same rule applied. A hug. An apology. All better.

Simple.

When did things become so complicated? When did I stop being able to simply hug and forgive? When did I feel only anger and confusion?

I am tormented by thoughts of the selfish, narcissistic, and manipulative man who has hurt me and taken everything from me. Hug and forgive? No! Why should he be able to walk away pain-free, head held high? Where is the justice? How can I forgive this six-foot, green-eyed, care-free, smooth-talking man, who came into my life and turned it upside down, leaving me to clean up the mess?

To begin... me, an ambitious young lady. Only 4'11" on a good day, but with fire and passion shining in my hazel eyes. I graduated high school with honors, top ten of my class, working two jobs, going to college, and maintaining a 3.5 GPA. Living away from my family, being independent. That was me. Independent. Fierce. I saved enough money to pay for my very own first car...in cash.

I was on top of the world. I was going to make it in this life, and nothing was going to stand in my way.

I was living in Colorado, attending college, away from my parents and siblings. At that moment in my life, I could do ANYTHING; be anything.

One day at work, Charlie approached me in a way he hadn't before. I could tell he liked me by the way he was being all flirty with me. I wasn't surprised when he asked me to go out with him. I ignored the warning flags. He was years older than me. It was very unprofessional. But I felt on top of the world, like nothing could go wrong in life. He was tall, slender, and handsome. He had a smile that could make you blush. But I wasn't worried. After all, he was just a guy. If things didn't work out, I would stop seeing him. Simple.

Shortly after we started dating, my living arrangements changed. My roommate decided to move out and waited until "moving day" to tell me. Just like that, I was homeless. I was mortified. I knew I couldn't let my family—or anyone—know. If my mother found out, she would make me come home immediately.

When Charlie discovered my secret, he offered to share his home with me. I said no. I knew better. Things were moving too fast for that. And then, a few weeks later, he asked me to marry him!

I found him attractive, but I did not love him. His offer caught me completely off guard. No, I told him. Don't be silly. We hardly know each other.

He said he knew I was confused but he insisted that he loved me, that he would care for me and keep me safe. Life would be beautiful. I still said no. But he asked again, and then again. Finally, I accepted and agreed to marry him.

How could I not? In truth, I was in no position to refuse. Besides, I thought, what could go wrong? I thought that Charlie must truly love me. He would not fight for me this hard if it wasn't real. Surely other people had love stories like this. Perhaps I was just fortunate enough to find such a wonderful man at nineteen.

It would be selfish of me to not grab the "brass ring!"

I began to tell everyone I knew about my relationship and to be more "wife-like" every day. Anything he needed, I was going to be the person that was there for him and I wanted him to know I meant it.

We moved in together right away and began planning our lives together. I expressed wanting a house with a dog and that perfect fairytale ending. White picket fence, happy smiles as we grow old together, all of it. But then, he said he wanted a child. I told him I was much too young to handle such a responsibility.

Why do people wait to have children, he wanted to know. All we need is a home, a career, support from our families, and each other.

To my mind, he made perfect sense.

At the time, I began working with his mother who had started her own skin care business. Talk about job security! He told me he'd looked at a house that could soon be ours. And he even surprised me with a puppy!

I was going to have it all! Of course I would have a child...

Months into my pregnancy, things changed. He began staying out later and no longer invited me places with him. I was confused and hurt. What had I done? He was hardly ever home and when he was, he didn't seem to have much time for me. Maybe he just had to get it out of his system before the baby was born—whatever "it" was.

But things didn't change. They only got worse. He stayed out later and later, sometimes not coming home at all. He lied about being at work. He drank from morning until night. I felt lost and confused. But this man was the father of my child and I was determined to make this work.

I thought counseling would work. I even went to Christian counseling because surely they would tell us to make things work. He went, kicking and screaming, but he went. Once there, he said he wanted to speak to the pastor alone, so he did.

Later that evening, the pastor called and counseled me to leave him.

What?

He told me it wasn't safe for me, that he would send people to help me move. What kind of pastor would say this? What was happening? Soon after this, Charlie crashed my car—he was driving drunk—and totaled it. Then he told me that he was going to move roommates into the house and that I would have to leave.

What?

I was panicked, angry, and scared. I didn't know what was happening. Who had he become? When had we stopped planning our wedding and life together? Shortly after, his mom said it wasn't a good idea for me to work with her if Charlie and I were not going to be together.

Just like that, my world was spiraling out of control.

My sister came to visit, and she couldn't believe this is what my life had become in such a short time. She began packing for me and informed my entire family back home that I could not stay here any longer. When I resisted, she got in my face. "You have a child to think about now! It's not just about you," she told me.

Of course, she was right. I was out of options. I had to go back and allow my family to help me. I cried. I sobbed. I didn't want to be such a failure. How had this happened so fast?

I hated Charlie for everything he had done, mostly for taking away that young woman who was so sure and determined. He betrayed me in the most cruel way. What kind of evil was he? I left. I took my child and he never came fighting for either one of us.

I was marked as a failure, instead of the bright, optimistic girl I'd been. Instead of the accomplished young woman making it on her own, I would now be forever looked at as a young single mother who ruined her life. This was a dark cloud over me.

If God was in charge of everything then why was he allowing this to happen? My heart was pure. I had nothing but good intentions and had done nothing wrong.

I hated Charlie with a passion. I hated the world...this was unfair. But then, one day when I thought I could never forgive him, I did.

* * *

A year had passed since I heard from Charlie. My heart still felt pain. One day a friend said to me, "You cannot hold on to a piece of hot coal and expect the other person to get burned." At that moment I realized that all the time and tears I had wasted wishing and praying for justice to be served, I had really been hurting myself. I had never let go of that pain and the truth was, I was tired of holding on to it. In that moment, I decided I had to change. I said one last prayer for Charlie, and I asked God to allow his will to be done—whatever that may be. I trusted that what was meant to be would be.

Having said my prayer, I got to work. No more sad songs. I only listened to music that lifted me up. I only viewed movies that would keep me feeling good and positive. I started to spend more time with church friends and family members that were supportive and full of good energy. I became totally forward looking. I focused on my new life and the new journey I would soon embark on. I stopped allowing myself to look back and worry about what I may have missed and began to look forward and get excited about all of the great things that may come.

People who hurt others usually are hurt themselves. For Charlie to have hurt me so deeply meant he must have been hurt a thousand times worse. I felt sorry for him. He would never know his beautiful, full-faced, smiling, chubby baby boy!

Charlie would never know what life he turned his back on. He would never know how to allow someone to love him. I prayed for him.

Years later, I heard from his mother that he had lived the same scenario several times. That made me sad. Not for me, but for him. I hope one day he will find God. In the meantime, I will not carry his burden.

My story is not a negative memory but a miraculous one of survival. And hope. If I can forgive...anyone can.

It really is that simple.

9

PASTOR BRAD
Fathers, I Forgive You

As a young boy, I looked up to my dad. He once told me, "Brad, I will never let you down and I will always be there for you."

These words play out in my mind nearly every waking day, and often in my imagination even when I sleep. When they do, I wake up suddenly. Thoughts of my dad run through my head. My heart pounds. He's alive! He's alive! Isn't he...?

I'd woken up to this same dream for years. I would be driving my car and, coming to a stoplight, I would look over and see my father in his Cordoba. It was so *him*. Looking like Burt Reynolds with his dark hair and darker skin, and 1970's sunglasses.

"Dad! Dad! It's me! I'm right here!" I'd yell as I frantically rolled down my window. He would look at me, expressionless. Then he'd turn back to the light and the road ahead, and he would drive away.

Waking up from this dream, I would have to remind myself that it was just a dream, that he really was gone. He was not there.

I had always been close with my father. We would go camping many weekends. When we couldn't get away, we would sit out in our backyard and sing songs that he played on his guitar. I couldn't help but believe we had the best family in the world. We camped. We sang. Dad worked hard for us, to help my brother and I reach our dreams.

When I was around five, my brother and I got into badminton. We would set up a makeshift net and play for hours. In our minds, we were going to win the Olympic badminton championship. One day we asked our dad if we could turn the entire backyard into a badminton court. This was no small deal as we would have to put sand in the entire backyard.

He raised an eyebrow at that.

"It's better to play barefoot," we explained.

"Hmm."

The next weekend my grandfather and father had a dump truck filled with sand show up. Working together, we got the sand into the backyard. My brother and I had our court. Once again, my father came through, encouraging our dreams.

After badminton, it was swimming.

"Dad, can we have a pool?"

He raised his eyebrows. But, to our joy and surprise, he got us the biggest above-ground pool he could. Within the week, we were swimming in our own backyard.

After that, we wanted a motorboat. By the end of the year, he bought a thirty-foot, two-decker boat and every weekend we all motor boated to Catalina Island and went fishing. Or, if that was too long a trip, we'd just motor around Newport Beach Harbor.

Time after time, my father proved to be my hero. He was always there for me.

What I didn't know then was that he loved alcohol. Really loved it. As a child, I didn't see a problem. However, the older I was, the worse his drinking seemed to become. He was what I came to understand a working-class alcoholic. He could drink all night, every day, and still managed to maintain a high-paying job.

More and more and more.

When I was ten, he divorced my mother and left her for another woman. His drinking turned into alcoholism.

He died at age forty-three.

When his life ended, it felt like mine did as well. My father, my hero, was gone. He promised me that he would be there for me, but he broke his promise. The fun-loving, creative, guitar playing dad...was now gone. The dad who poured sand into the backyard for his badminton-playing sons was gone. The dad who took us out in the motorboat, gone.

He left me.

He broke his promise.

Not long after, my mother began dating a man who eventually became our stepdad. He was a deep-sea diver. What boy wouldn't have been won over by him? I loved sports, surfing, running, and more. So, this adventurous guy completely won me over. I went diving with him and was able to get my diver's license from him at age twelve. I even made my first night dive and went seventy feet down on the backside of the Santa Cruz Islands, off the Northern California coast.

I bonded with him. I was a boy and I needed a father in my life. I was still angry that my real father, my hero, was gone. I even asked my stepdad to be my dad. To my surprise and disappointment he said, "Brad, I had kids and I do not want anymore. I cannot and will not be your father. You are your mother's kids." He also asked me to call him by his first name. "We can be friends," he said.

I was devastated. I didn't want a friend. I wanted a dad. I needed a dad. My life began to spiral out of control. The pain of rejection led me to seek out a way to drown out my pain. I started to make friends with all the wrong kids and began a life of drugs and alcohol. I was a young teenager who was lost, rejected and hurt by my father and stepfather.

When I was seventeen, my fun-loving mother, who was also my best friend, told me she was moving to Mexico with my stepdad. She didn't want to lose him and felt she needed him to take care of her.

"So, we're moving to Mexico?" I asked.

She shook her head. She told me I could not go and that I needed to find a place to live. I ended up living in my car in front of my friend's house. I was a very good kid with many gifts and talents but was hurt by my father and stepfather's rejection and abandonment. In my heart of hearts, I believed they both let me down. I had deep hurt and anger for them. My father died and let me down. My stepfather didn't want me and took my mother away from me.

For the next eight years, I followed in my father's footsteps. I was a working-class drug addict and alcoholic just like he was. The unforgiveness in my heart eventually caused me to lose my job. I was fast approaching rock bottom. It wasn't until I was twenty-five that my life finally began to turn around. It was then that I met the father I really wanted and needed all my life.

It was in a seedy hotel room. I'd been up for several days, strung out on drugs with my girlfriend. At the time, I didn't know that she was a backslidden Christian. I'd gone out with her for two years but never knew she was a believer. Even if I knew, I wouldn't have known what it meant. "Christian" was just another label to me. Jesus meant nothing to me. But at some point during that weekend, in that seedy hotel room, she pulled a Bible from a drawer and held it in my face. "Brad, you need Jesus."

Understand, like me she had been up for many days, strung out on drugs. I looked at the book, shrugged my shoulders, and said, "Okay." I hadn't said it with any real conviction and yet as soon as I said it, I felt this power come into my life. I fell to the ground and began crying for a half hour. When I finally stopped crying, I got up off the ground and realized something. I was no longer high, drunk, stoned, or tired. For the first time in a long time I was free. I felt I was no longer addicted to drugs or alcohol.

God was in my life. God was with me.

That night, when I accepted Jesus into my life, He introduced me to someone who wanted to be my Father. Jesus introduced me to my heavenly Father. Finally, I had a Father who would never turn His back on me, never reject me, never break His promise to me.

God literally became my Father. I spent hours in prayer with Him as He taught me through His word and through speaking to my heart how to be a real man...a godly man. One day, God spoke to my heart and said, "Brad, you must forgive your father and stepfather."

I wanted to, but I did not know how. Then God spoke to my heart and helped me understand that, just as He had forgiven me for my many sins and for denying Him for so long, so too I had to forgive.

It was then that I understood forgiveness. I spoke my forgiveness out loud and when I did, God did something in my heart. He healed it. He released me from my pain of rejection and abandonment. Forgiveness! What a gift. It was only when I released my "unforgiveness" that I was truly free. I was no longer consumed with hurt or rejection. I was free; free to embrace God and His plan for me.

And the dreams that had woken me so many nights in a heart-thumping, cold sweat? Shortly after receiving Christ, I sat on the edge of my bed still feeling hurt, anger, and pain in my heart. I so desperately wanted God to remove my pain. So, I took a leap of faith. "Father, I want to forgive and release my dad and stepdad to you. I forgive them and I accept that they were somehow a part of your plan to draw me to you. Please take this pain away and replace it with your love and forgiveness."

I immediately felt God's presence fill my heart. There was no longer any room for the pain I had been carrying for so many years. The bad dreams stopped. Four words relieved me of my terrible burden: Fathers, I Forgive You!

SANDRA
My Journey of Forgiving a Serious Medical Error

How do you turn a "blind eye" to someone responsible for you losing your sight?

Twenty-five years ago, I was diagnosed with glaucoma. For the first few years, the condition was controlled with eye drops. When the drops stopped being successful, my doctor put a "bleb" in both eyes to act as a filtration device. Then, nearly five years ago, the pressure in my eye began to rise. The bleb had scarred over. Once again, my doctor had me using various eye drops. Back and forth I went to him, trusting him, relying on him. Even when I started losing peripheral vision, I kept going to him.

Finally, he sent me to a specialist who took one read of the pressure in my eye and scheduled me for surgery the very next day, hoping to save my vision. Unfortunately, I ended up losing most of my vision in that, my good eye.

I could no longer drive. I found myself falling over things I couldn't see. I relied on large-print books to read. I was horrified to need my husband to tell me who people were because I could no longer distinguish facial features well.

I grew bitter as the list of my "disabilities" grew and I grew angry with the doctor who caused this to happen to me.

"You just have to accept where you are," my husband told me. But even as I struggled to accept and accommodate my blindness, I could not fathom forgiving the doctor whom I'd trusted and who had betrayed that trust.

* * *

One day, my pastor's wife invited me to a luncheon at our church. I didn't often go to these types of luncheons but when she told me that there would be a speaker there talking about her book on forgiveness, I was intrigued. I even read the book beforehand. Her words spoke to my heart. Then, when I heard her speak her story of how she'd found a way to forgive abandonment, childhood molestation, racism, bullying, and domestic violence, I was moved to my core. I went up to her after the luncheon and told her I needed forgiveness intervention.

How could I have known, as I confessed to her how moved I'd been by her book, that she had prayed that very morning and God had placed in her spirit that a woman would come to her after the luncheon and speak to her about forgiveness. She said God had laid on her heart to write down four tools of forgiveness to give to a woman after the luncheon.

* * *

It happened that several days before the luncheon, my blindness bothered me so deeply that I felt compelled to call my former eye doctor. I was determined to let him know how his negligence had damaged my life. I was not able to speak with him but his receptionist gave me an appointment to come in to speak with him, an appointment which was, as it happened, three days after the luncheon.

My coming appointment weighed on my heart as I spoke with the author. I knew our meeting could be no coincidence; it had to have been divinely ordered. She opened her notebook and took out a blue Post-it with the date of the luncheon and four tools of forgiveness.

"These," she said, "are for you."

I looked at the Post-it and read:

1. Be honest about what happened.
2. Be willing to let go of your unforgiveness baggage.
3. Take time to forgive yourself.
4. Embrace your rebirth.

At that moment, I knew God had a better plan for my life, and I was open to His voice. As the author had forgiven those responsible for the traumas in her life, God was calling on me to forgive my doctor.

I knew I could not continue to live with the rage in my heart. I had to trust in God.

Patiently, the author explained each step, and then prayed for me. Now, with this counsel and my trust in God, I was ready to meet with my doctor. I had planned on going to my appointment with a list of the ways the doctor had ruined my life. But God had a better plan. I was honest. I was direct. But

I spoke with peace in my heart rather than rage. I told him, "Your negligence changed my life. I need to hear you say that you're sorry."

He did apologize and I said that I forgave him—and I did. We hugged, and I left the office, no longer carrying my unforgiveness baggage.

* * *

Since that appointment, my physical blindness has continued to be a challenge. I have fallen, run into things, and failed to recognize people. But not once have I felt anger in my heart. Forgiveness has taken care of that. Now I am in control of the quality of my life. Someone else's mistake does not define me. It is true, there are things I can no longer do, but I have God and forgiveness in my heart. I have a wonderful life, thanks to the Lord, and thanks to the author who showed me a better way, a way freed from the burden of bitterness and regret.

My forgiveness healed me, not my doctor.

Forgiveness is for my heart.

It is a lesson worth learning.

The author who gave me the tools and prayed for me after the luncheon is the author of this book.

GLORIA
Breaking the Cycle of Sexual Molestation

When you forgive, you set yourself free. When you give yourself permission to let go of anger and embrace laughter, hope, and goodness, you're releasing yourself from the shackles that bind you and you are embracing freedom. Forgiveness is empowering; it is about taking back your power.

Gloria Ewing Lockhart, *Unmasking: A Woman's Journey* [4]

I was eight when my adopted mother, Frances, had to travel out of town to care for her parents who had been in a car accident. She left me in the care of my adopted father, Harry. Dad was a prominent and respectful minister, and he took care of me when Mom was away.

He was a caring and nurturing man until one night, there was a terrible storm. When I close my eyes, I can still hear the roar of the wind and rain. The hail pounded so hard against the house that I was frightened someone was trying to break in. Terrified, I pulled my blankets over my head to feel safe. But I was even more terrified under the blankets. I cried out to my dad...

That night, after I slid into his bed for my own comfort, he crossed the line that can never be re-crossed. He held me in his arms a bit too tightly. He whispered in my ear a bit too urgently. He touched me.

This man, who had once lifted me so high into the sky that I thought I would bang my head against the heavens, who had defended me and provided for me when my biological father wouldn't, who had spoken truth to so many, was now the cause of all that shattered within me.

Those big, strong hands once so comforting, now so frightening.

My molestation was a forty-year secret, spoken to no one, not even God in the prayers could I find the strength to utter. Through the years, I replayed the events of that stormy night. If only my biological mom had kept me. If only, if only, if only... I was obsessed with "ifs" and "what ifs."

I never again trusted Dad Harry, but I never felt hate toward him. I wasn't even angry with him. The reason was simple, I never blamed him. I saved my anger, hate, and blame for myself.

This horrible secret weighed heavy on me, until finally, I could no longer bear it. I was sure I would lose my mind if I didn't purge myself of this pain and yet the only way out that I could imagine was if I took my own life. That seemed to be the only sure way for this torture to finally end.

My Christian faith had taught me to forgive; gave me the strength to overcome other hurts in my life—I was able to forgive the other things that cut so deeply into my soul. I could forgive my natural parents for abandoning me, I could forgive the bullies who pelted me with rocks, I could forgive my husband for his abuse of me, I could even forgive the pain of the racism ignorant Whites inflicted upon me. But to forgive this, this horrific deepest sin tested my faith to the point of breaking.

I didn't even know how to give voice to the horror of that abuse. I was at a dark, paralyzing state. I could only challenge Him; *Where were you when it happened? Why didn't you stop it?*

My path to forgiveness began during an exceptional moment, looking into my young daughter's eyes. In those sparkling, brown eyes there were no storms, no anger, no hurt, just joy, trust, and innocence. I saw in those eyes so much of what I wanted to wholly embrace again. In those eyes, I felt God's presence and I saw a way forward. I had to live, and live fully. For her.

I could not end my life. I could not leave her to live her life without me, to always question and wonder; Why? I could not leave her with such hurt and the lesson that the way to deal with your problems is to run.

In that moment, I took a first step forward. I began to speak to people who felt hurt and hopeless; I tried to understand them, and through them, understand myself. I heard in their voices and their stories a desire to find love, to find someone to listen to their stories, someone to intervene.

I began to understand that it wasn't my fault.

From my own experience, and the experiences of others, I developed "Six Steps of Forgiveness"—a plan that can be applied to your life and journey. Using these steps, I was able to find my way forward and to forgive. Using these steps, you can do the same.

I have created these steps from my years of social work, my personal experiences in life, and my walk with Jesus. It is not necessary to experience these steps sequentially. All you have to do is begin to practice forgiveness one step at a time. After all, that's what a journey is.

To embrace these steps, keep in mind that if we expect God to forgive us, then the same practice should apply to forgiving others.

Step I: Forgiveness is a Journey, not a Sprint

Whatever you are holding onto in this life, hold it loosely so it won't hurt when the Lord has to pry your fingers open to take it away. – Priscilla Shirer[5]

Inevitably, it has taken you years to reach the point where you are ready to begin your journey to forgiveness. That is a great distance to travel and like all great distances cannot be traveled in one headlong sprint. The journey to free yourself from anger, hate, revenge, bitterness, guilt, grudges, and hopelessness covers a lot of ground. You won't shed unforgiveness overnight; it has taken years to creep into your psyche and spirit. Being able to rid the unforgiveness can only be done one step at a time. Realize that this journey, like all others, is valuable not only for reaching the end but for the joy and beauty found along the way. So in recognizing this, begin your journey with an open heart. When you do, you will be open to hear the voice of God speak to you. The healing process begins here because you put yourself in a vulnerable position with Him. He tells us in John 10:4 NIV, "When he has brought out all his own, he goes on ahead of them, and his sheep follow him because they know his voice."

Remember to listen only to the right voice, the voice that speaks God's truth, not to people who may exacerbate further unforgiveness. The right voice always aligns with the Word of God. The right voice always gives you hope. Ask the Holy Spirit to give you discernment of His voice. Walk closely with Him, and He will point you to His voice. The right voice tells you that, "I can do all things through Christ who strengthens me" (Philippians 4:13 NKJV).

I don't want you to think that forgiveness is easy. It's not. But there is no freedom and no joy without taking the journey to get to forgiveness. Like all journeys, each is different from another. In my case, because Dad Harry had passed away before I could talk to him, it was easier for me to turn away from my need to forgive. After all, there was no one to approach to give forgiveness to. But, no matter how hard I tried to turn away, no matter how hard I tried to forget, I could not. My memory, my self-hate, my self-blame, and my hurt showed itself in a thousand different ways—in my sense of shame, in my self-destructive thoughts, and in my behavior.

Forty years!

That's how long my journey took. That is too long.

One of the reasons it took so long was that I was always told, *"Forgive, forget, and move on with your life."* But those are only words. It is not a simple task to forgive. Mine was deep so there was no way I could simply dismiss what had happened. In general, the sooner we can forgive, the healthier. The less time for the hurt, blame, and guilt to fester, the less healing required.

No matter how old the injury, it must be forgiven. And, like any journey, forgiveness can only be accomplished one step at a time.

Step 2: Identify the Experience...Break the Silence

Instead of shame and dishonor, you will inherit a double portion of prosperity and everlasting joy (Isaiah 61:7 NLT).

Nothing is more frightening than silence. Fear keeps us paralyzed. To break silence is to do the bravest thing possible.

Breaking silence is cathartic—it allows you to get your negative feelings *out* from where they are locked within you. Of course, it is not enough simply to express those feelings but it is a necessary first step to *deal* with them. Talk to a trusted friend, to your minister, or to a counselor. The things that must be said to break the silence are answers to these questions:

1. What happened?
2. When did it happen?
3. Where did it happen?

This first step is so hard but I promise you, you will begin to feel relief the moment you are able to break free from the silence. When I finally determined to free myself from my silence, I sat for a full hour before I could utter a single word. An hour! I had forty years of silence to overcome; forty years of shame, guilt, and self-blame. But as soon as I was able to speak that first word, the pressure began to ease. My face was aflame in shame because I had blamed myself for forty years, but my heart was lighter as soon as I began to speak.

Until you find the courage to speak to break the silence, the heavier the burden becomes. But once you break your silence, you're no longer a prisoner to the shackles of unforgiveness.

In breaking your silence, there's something else important here. It's the grieving process. I strongly recommend that we go through this because some of us have shackles of unforgiveness that may be traumatic. Give yourself time to grieve. When we don't, we often suppress the trauma deep into our psyche where we rehearse it as I did for forty years. Eventually the trauma turns into destructive behavior like anger, bitterness, low self-esteem, fear, and even hate. For me, the trauma of being molested had grown so deep, I was numb. I questioned living. In *The Journey: Forgiveness, Restorative Justice and Reconciliation*, authors Stephanie Hixon and Thomas Porter, remind us of the importance of grieving to heal: "We cannot heal what we cannot feel. We need time to feel our pain and loss and all the emotions and tears that surround them. As we mourn and grieve we start the journey of healing the wound...This journey has many rhythms—whether weeping and wailing with dances and shouts or tending to details of burial rites, or prayerfully writing out our hearts in our journal, or exercising vigorously to release rage and pain—these and many more are expressions of lament and mourning."[6]

Step 3: Take Inventory of Who You Are

Choosing forgiveness is one of the most difficult things God asks us to do, especially if we believe that whoever hurt us is in the wrong and doesn't deserve to be forgiven. But God instructs us to practice forgiveness. And when we choose to follow the path of forgiveness, we will experience the peace and joy that come through obeying God's Word.
– Joyce Meyer [7]

The past is always *behind you*. Be forward looking. Focus on positive messages and habits that can change your life, not on the past negative messages that darkened your past. Focus on your life ahead, not on the time that has been lost.

Try this exercise—take a piece of paper and draw a line down the middle. On the left side, write *Things that block my success*, and on the right side write *Things that keep me going*. In the right column, list the personal strengths that have allowed you to make it through life through every obstacle. My own list of strengths included my faith, thoughts of the people in my family who had overcome long odds from the 1800s to present, successes in track and field, and acquiring an education. You certainly have as many or more such strengths. Acknowledge them. Embrace them. Here is an ideal place to list ten victories that you've accomplished over your lifetime. Now, speak them out loud. They will help when you question your self-esteem.

Now, on the left side under *Things that block my success*, list the obstacles that have hindered you. Some of my own obstacles included fear of abandonment, low self-esteem, and anger.

The left side showed me the things I had to work on in order to move into forgiveness. The right side showed me the things that would allow me to get there.

Step 4: Forgive Yourself

To forgive is to set a prisoner free and discover that the prisoner was you. – Lewis B. Smedes [8]

Forgiveness is a decision. It doesn't just happen. It is a choice we make, a choice to let go of our past hurts. Fundamental to that choice is our understanding that we cannot have a better past. The past is gone. It's over. The good news is that we have hope in the future. What we do today will impact our future.

Forgiveness means, first and foremost, forgiving ourselves; forgiving ourselves of internalizing blame, shame, and low self-esteem; forgiving ourselves for carrying the weight of secrets and hurt for which we were not to blame. Forgiveness means recognizing that we are all worthy of being freed of our pain and hurt. If God is willing to forgive us for our sins against Him, certainly we can forgive ourselves for our sins against ourselves.

Try some of these exercises to learn how to forgive yourself.

1. Stand in front of the mirror for the next month and, each day, repeat these words: *"I love (your name). I forgive the pain I've inflicted on me that caused me to feel bad about who I am. I'm confident. I'm a victor not a victim because I can do all things through Christ who strengthens me."*

2. Write a letter to yourself, expressing your pain. Nothing is too dark or too wrong to be forgiven. Then, with a dear friend, conduct a ceremony during which you burn your letter. If you have actually wronged someone, reach out to them and ask for their forgiveness. If that person is not available, do what you must to forgive yourself. Forgiveness is for you. It's an ongoing act.

Step 5: Forgive Others

I think the hardest thing in life is to forgive. Hate is self-destructive. If you hate somebody, you're not hurting the person you hate, you're hurting yourself. It's a healing, actually, it's a real healing...forgiveness. – Louis Zamperini [9]

For many people, this is the step that causes them the most difficulty. Even if they have managed to forgive themselves, forgiving the one who caused them such hurt is a monumental step. Often, our hearts wish pain and suffering on those who have hurt us. Our hearts cry out for retribution and justice.

This is human and understandable.

Unfortunately, these feelings will not allow us to move forward in our lives. Our desire for retribution torments our own hearts and souls. Only forgiveness releases us, only forgiveness allows us to move forward in our own lives. I understand how hard this step is. I had so much to forgive—my biological parents for abandoning me, my adoptive father for molesting me, my teachers for demeaning me. It wasn't until I understood that holding on to my desire to punish those who had harmed me was hurting *me* more than it was hurting them that I was able to move forward.

Perhaps as importantly, how do we actually move forward to forgive?

I found the following to be helpful:

1. *Sit quietly, meditate, and pray.*

Meditation is practiced throughout the Bible. It allows you to move deep into your heart and thoughts to better understand your pain; to consider Scriptures that will address what you're going through. It will open your heart to the wisdom of God, the blessings and benefits of forgiving others. Forgiving others should be based on how Christ so freely forgives us as found in Matthew 6:12 GNT: "If you forgive others the wrongs they have done to you, your Father in heaven will also forgive you."

As you meditate, it's normal to revisit the source of your hurt. You may cry or become angry or even question God. These are normal reactions. Meditation allows you to revisit your emotions with the goal to *release* negative emotions.

It's important to know that you may or may not be able to come face-to-face with the person who has wronged you, but your true obligation is to let go of your pain, hate, resentment, and anger so that you can embrace peace. Prayer is also help-ful; it allows time to commune with God. It allows us to break down our stubborn will so that we can humbly submit our peti-tion to God for restoration.

2. *Let go of the anger.*

Anger held on to hardens into hate and bitterness. Eventu-ally it might manifest itself in the form of ill health. Holding on to our anger is just a way to protect ourselves, to guard our hurt and vulnerability in the confused notion that doing so protects us from more pain. It doesn't.

In an article, "Forgiveness: Your Health Depends on It," Karen Swartz, MD of Johns Hopkins Hospital speaks to how unforgiveness can impact the body over time: "Chronic anger puts you into a fight-or-flight mode, which results in numerous changes in heart rate, blood pressure and immune response. Those changes, then, increase the risk of depression, heart dis-ease and diabetes, among other conditions. Forgiveness, how-ever, calms stress levels, leading to improved health."[10]

Only forgiveness protects us by releasing that which is de-structive to us from lurking within our own hearts.

3. *Take the high road.*

Forgiveness is not weakness but power, the power to heal. It is the power to have compassion not only for ourselves but for the ones who have harmed us.

Remember, if there is retribution that is to be had, and if it is justifiable, then God will attend to it. You don't need to worry about it.

Make forgiveness manageable for you. For some, addressing the person who has caused them harm face-to-face is most powerful; for others, writing a letter or some other form of communication is best. Sometimes, as in my case, you can no longer address the person who has hurt you. You should then forgive them through prayer and in your own heart.

Forgiveness is for you, find a way to make it happen!

Step 6: Dream and Soar

"For I know the plans I have for you," declares the Lord, "plans to prosper you and not to harm you, plans to give you hope and a future" (Jeremiah 29:11 NIV).

Just as an eagle flies above storms, we were born to rise high above our pain. Without the weight of our unforgiveness, we can soar high above the clouds; we can heal.

As we begin to heal, we begin to dream anew. The future is a reality that can be affected by our thoughts and actions. Giving voice to dreams will take time. Perhaps a support group or a few friends who believe in you can help you sort through those dreams. Gather with others whose focus in the future will help you train yourself to look forward and not backward. This is the time to expand your vision, go beyond your circumstances, and walk continually with Him so you can hear His voice direct you. Habakkuk 2:2-3, NKJV, leaves us with instruction: "Write the vision. And make it plain on tablets, that he may run who reads it. For the vision is yet for an appointed time; But at the end it will speak, and it will not lie. Though it tarries, wait for it; Because it will surely come, It will not tarry."

Make a goal. Make specific ways to achieve it. To help me with my goals, my daughter suggested creating a Vision Board from magazine pictures and large letters with my goals. Post it in a visible spot. Spend fifteen minutes a day implementing your steps and working on goals. Once a goal is achieved, go on to the next! In no time, you will know that your destiny is yours to achieve.

God has planted dreams in you to fulfill His purpose.

This is the time when you'll want to inspire others through your story. Volunteer at your church or with an organization. As you recreate the "new you," build on your successes. Plan on returning to school; prepare for a new, challenging, different job, or travel for missions inside the United States and beyond. I attended graduate school in social work so that I could help others realize their possibilities. Challenging myself, I became one of the first African American women to reach the summit of Mt. Kilimanjaro!

No matter what you've been through, God will begin to bless you beyond measure because you've fulfilled His promise of forgiveness.

CAROL
Forgiving My Low Self-Esteem and Unwanted Pregnancies

I was attracted to Christopher because he was handsome with fine features. A biker and a vet, I met him at a Christmas party. He was 5'10" but seemed taller. His teeth were bad from his time in the army.

He liked me because I was a White girl with a big butt. A "good" Catholic girl, I liked him because he liked and wanted me. We married a year after meeting, in 1978. I was twenty-one. Thomas, our son, was born nine months later. You can do the math.

I hoped that having a beautiful little baby would help free my husband from his demons. His time in Vietnam had left him an alcoholic and addicted to crystal meth. But having a son didn't change him at all.

A year after our son was born, I was pregnant again. But I did not give birth to a second child. Instead of a baby, I carried with me a secret, one that has burrowed into my soul for all these years. I had an abortion.

Christopher was all for the abortion. In fact, he'd wanted me to get an abortion with our first child but I'd refused. As a Catholic, I was taught to be married if I carried a child. So Christopher and I had married. But now? My marriage was in danger. Christopher didn't work so I was the only one bringing in an income. He was abusive to me psychologically. He was unstable. I couldn't trust him alone with the baby.

I knew it was wrong, but I couldn't have another baby.

I knew it was a sin to take a life. I knew abortion is against the teachings of the church. I knew other women had bad marriages, marriages that were even worse than mine. But they had their children. This weighed heavily on me.

Second child or not, my marriage could not survive. The alcohol and meth were bad. But he also carried a .357 Magnum in the back of his pants. He often talked of suicide and of taking me and my son with him. I couldn't stay anymore. After eight years of abuse, we divorced.

I was twenty-nine when I met Sam, who would be my lover for the next twenty years. I had no illusions about him. He was a womanizer, and a musician. Six feet tall, dark skin, and shiny black hair. He was commanding and wonderful. We partied a lot, while still maintaining day jobs.

During our time together, I got pregnant a few times. Each time I did, someone in his family would remind me that Sam always had another woman and that he wouldn't be there, that he had other children that he didn't know, refused to know.

Children he didn't support. Exes that he didn't communicate with.

And, he could be abusive. He broke my nose twice. So, behind his back I had four abortions during the time we were together. Each time, I went to the clinic alone. Each time, I would come home alone. I would lie to him for the next few weeks, telling him I had a yeast infection or anything to excuse not having sex while I healed.

Finally, I stopped to ask myself, "Why do you keep doing this?" and I came to realize it was because I was living in fear. Fear of myself, fear of everything. I felt responsible for ending the life of these poor, innocent beings. I felt unworthy. I had made my decisions selfishly.

I came to see my horrible decisions in light of a childhood that had left me without any sense of self. My biological mother abandoned me at four, leaving for another man. She never came back for me or my brother. My father remarried and my stepmother beat us. I have few, if any, positive memories, but did that excuse what I'd done?

I was wracked with guilt and shame. Why didn't I carry those children? I couldn't trust their fathers. I didn't know how I would be able to support them. I didn't know if I'd have the strength. But were these only unfair excuses? Were they excuse enough to take life?

I was guilty and was sure I didn't deserve forgiveness.

From the time I graduated high school in 1975 until I was almost forty, I didn't step foot in a Catholic church. My life was broken. I knew that. And I was desperate for answers. But I didn't reach out for them. I saw Christians at work who served the Lord and I saw that they had a relationship with God, something I never had. They told me they would pray for me, and they brought me Bibles. They cared and wanted to teach me a better way of thinking about myself.

They invited me to their church in the South Bay. Sometimes I went but I still struggled because I felt I didn't belong among good people, among Christians. It took me a long time but something from the church and being around Christians began to affect me.

I began to open each day with prayer, asking the Lord to forgive me, to take away my guilt. I spoke the words but I didn't feel forgiveness because I had not forgiven myself. I tried to compensate for my low self-esteem and my many sins. I tried to raise myself up. After all, I had a good job. I'd never stolen. I hadn't committed a crime in front of people. I tried to tell myself maybe what I'd done wasn't so bad.

But sin is sin, no matter what you do. And, no sin is greater than another. "For all have sinned and fall short of the glory of God" (Romans 3:23 NKJV).

I had used abortion as a form of birth control. I had sinned. I could not undo what I'd done. Now my biggest challenge was ridding myself of guilt.

I continued to go to church. I listened to the Word. I tried to allow God's Holy Spirit to soak into my soul. Sharing with others who have guilt as I have, helped me deeply.

Prayer after prayer, year after year, I kept asking Jesus to forgive me, *but it was me who never forgave myself.* He has forgiven me the minute I ask for forgiveness, as His word has as-sured me: "He has removed our sins as far from us as the east is from the west" (Psalms 103:12 NLT). Even now, to this day, I am still working on forgiving myself.

It was the teachings of Joyce Meyer that finally opened my eyes. She expressed the same repetitive request in her prayers for Jesus to forgive her sins. She expressed guilt and shame of being abused and enduring it for many years. She moved for-ward by allowing the Holy Spirit to work in her life to remove shame. I have sought God's spirit to do the same in my life for the gift of forgiveness. She shared that Jesus told her that he had already forgiven her the first time she asked.

I took that into my heart, and I told myself to let go of what I cannot undo; I told myself that to not forgive myself is to not believe in the blood that Jesus shed on the cross for me. I had no choice but to forgive myself and give it back to Jesus to help me forget and move forward and mature to feel whole.

* * *

Each day, as I drive two hours to work, I listen to the Word, and day-by-day forgiveness sinks in a bit deeper. I know that I have to be open to forgiving myself, lest I sabotage my own for-giveness. This realization prompted me to reach out to other women to help them overcome their guilt. Self-anger and self-hate paralyze us all. It was only when I forgave myself that I found relief.

A concrete step I took in my healing forgiveness was to name each child I aborted and to place those names in my Bible. I look forward to meeting them when Jesus takes me home. Praise the Lord.

Forgiveness is real. Forgiveness is immediate. But forgiveness is not a quick fix. Everyone has a different way of getting unforgiveness out of their head as I did, but today I can finally say, I have forgiven myself.

Find your way, but forgive.

"Therefore, if anyone is in Christ, he is a new creation; old things have passed away; behold, all things have become new" (2 Corinthians 5:17 NKJV).

BRIAN
Who's Fault Is It? I'm Now Living With Diabetes

Not long ago, I was diagnosed with diabetes II. My immediate thought was, Way to go. You finally ate yourself into a disease that's going to kill you.

Great.

From my earliest years, I have been the type of person who would eat my emotions away rather than confront them. I would do this even though I knew the futility of it. As soon as the food was gone, the depression or anxiety remained.

Food had always been a focus in my home. When my mother was a child, she grew up poor and there were too many times when she went to bed hungry. Because of her experience, she made sure that her little boys never experienced what she had to go through. As a result, I grew up in a house filled with candy bars and potato chips.

I was taught from a very early age that food equaled happiness and security. And, in this lesson, I was a model student.

When I finally came to understand my damaging relationship with food, I was angry and upset with my mother. How could she do this to me? How could she not protect me from food? Why didn't she try to teach me how to eat sensibly?

Did we really need *every* brand of candy bar in the house?

I was angry with her and, finally, I was angry with myself. How could I, as a grown man, still blame my mother for my own poor choices? One night, alone in the darkness of my bedroom, I wept over her passing. As I wept, a moment of true clarity came to me and I whispered into the darkness of my room, "I forgive you, Mama. I forgive you for not teaching me how to eat. I love you for being there for me and feeding me."

It was a powerful relief, letting go of the anger and forgiving her. But, I quickly learned, that was only half the battle. I still had to forgive *myself* for not controlling my eating habits as an adult. That process turned out to be much more difficult and complex than I'd imagined. That path and process has become a constant in my life, a daily ritual as real and vital as breathing. My habit has become prayer, realizing that Jesus is walking with me, never giving up on me, never letting me down.

This path has led me to lose seventy pounds and I am looking forward to losing another seventy. Along the way, I have learned—and embraced—that I have a lot to live for. I have my son, my friends, and the clients who I have come to care for and have an investment in their progress. Each time I make a good food choice or exercise, I visualize my mother hugging and telling me, "I am so proud of you, honey."

In allowing forgiveness to fill up my heart, I allow myself to shine a little light in a darkened world.

GLORIA EWING LOCKHART

MONAE
My Journey From Hate to Forgiving My BFF's Husband

D'Ana was my best friend. Petite, barely five-feet tall, she was a beautiful young woman with caramel-colored skin and light brown eyes. She liked her hair short and sassy. I loved her like a dear sister.

Her choice in best friends was perfect. Her choice in husbands...not so much. She may have called him her dream man but the truth was he abused her verbally and physically. Tony could be charming but he also had a substance problem. She never wanted to talk about his cruelty but I could see her black eyes, and the bruises on her arms and body.

I was always the one watching out for her, ever since we were little girls. It wasn't just her size that made her a target. She was just so sweet and kind. I would beat anyone who messed with her or her family. I was her protector. She, of course, didn't like conflict but conflict always seemed to come looking for her.

I tried to help her and Tony. I tried talking. I tried arguing. Sometimes I even threatened him. But nothing I said seemed to have much effect. D'Ana mostly kept us apart, knowing that one day I would likely get into some type of altercation with him and end up in trouble myself. For a time, that meant she kept me at arm's length. I guess she didn't want to see me go to jail.

I'd have gladly gone if it would have kept her safe.

* * *

We both got saved in our early thirties and together we both grew closer to Jesus. We both started attending church regularly, working in church, and sharing what God had done for us. We helped feed the poor, worked in the children's ministry, and marriage ministry. Whatever was needed, we were there.

We felt the presence of the Lord in our lives.

Mostly our prayers got answered. And those that didn't, the praying helped us deal. Tony's abuse didn't stop, but D'Ana wouldn't stop trusting God for her life and her children's lives. I prayed along with her, hoping and believing for change in her life.

I told her that she had to stand up to him; that confronting him would make him respect her more. Well, one day she did exactly that. She hit him with her son's toy fire engine, which was nearly as big as she was. That got his attention. He did stop hitting her, but the verbal abuse didn't stop. He called her names that I can't repeat.

He tore her down mentally. My dear, kind, sweet friend became guarded and unsure. Still, her love for Jesus only got stronger. Sometimes, Tony would go to church with her. When the Holy Spirit touched her and she got to dancing in the Spirit and for Jesus, she wouldn't even remember, but he was sure to let her know; telling her she was dancing and looking like a fool.

When she moved to Lake Tahoe, she grew even closer to God. D'Ana would tell me that the house they were living in was way up in the mountains. She could see the top of the trees from her window. She told me she felt so close to God when she prayed because she was so high up the mountains.

It just seemed that the closer she got to God the more Tony got angry and was verbally abusive. She kept praying. He kept being abusive. She would wait until he left for work then fall to her knees where she began to pray.

One day, she just got tired of it all and said she wanted out. "Heaven's my way out," she told me.

Her words scared me. I told her not to say that. "You've got to be careful with what you say," I told her. Words are powerful, there is life and death in what one speaks.

I had visited her in Nevada in December. Oh, we had a wonderful time. We talked all night about God, her home, her family, joys and disappointments. She was tired. I just tried to encourage her heart.

Soon after that, she started having bad migraines. These were new so I told her to see a doctor. She said she would, but she said it would pass. Next thing I know, I got a phone call telling me she'd had a stroke, caused by an aneurysm in her brain.

She was rushed to a hospital in Nevada and then to a specialist in the Bay Area of California.

I rushed to be with her, in the Bay Area. I talked to her, laughed with her, and asked her if she wanted me to take care of her kids. Even as we laughed, my gut feeling was that I would not see her again.

I tried to pray with her alone. I just wanted to pray and believe God with her, but she wasn't having it. That was when I decided to go back home to San Pedro, California, and pray for her there. I called her before she was going in for surgery. I told her I loved her and I was praying. I wanted to hear her voice one last time. As soon as I said that I asked, Why did I say that? Why?

She never woke up after the surgery. But I wasn't going to give up. I wanted her to wake up. I was devastated, I was angry. I cried. I couldn't stop the tears. But through the tears, I prayed. I even fasted from food for three days so she would wake up. But she didn't wake up. I didn't know what else to do. I couldn't stop crying. When I did, I was angry. Why her, God? Why her?

I felt lost. I couldn't talk to her. I couldn't laugh and joke with her. NOTHING! NOTHING AT ALL!

She was in a coma for a year, then Tony had the feeding tube removed. She died three weeks later. I blamed him for her death and suffering. Her husband had them stop the tube, which was the only reason she was alive. He'd been so mean to her. I hated him for taking her away from me. She was my best friend and I failed her. Because of him, I couldn't help her. I couldn't protect her.

I asked God why He didn't take Tony instead of her. Oh, I was angry, angry. And I kept that anger in my heart for years. I would boil when his name was mentioned. My heart would break all over again. I felt a weight on me that I just couldn't get out from under. I would just start crying in the middle of the day.

How I wanted to hurt him like he hurt me and my friend.

Then one day, the Lord dropped in my spirit to forgive him. It was a small voice that I heard.

Forgive him? Never! My heart wouldn't allow it. Now, I knew from being in church how Jesus always spoke about love and forgiveness. And I was trying my best to live like Jesus. I knew I could never ever be like the Lord, but I wanted to do my best for Him. Jesus loves us so much. But it was hard to forgive Tony.

Then I happened to read the following scripture: "For if you forgive other people when they sin against you, your heavenly Father will also forgive you. But if you do not forgive others their sins, your Father will not forgive your sins" (Matthew 6:14-15 NIV).

There was a time when I really thought that I had forgiven Tony. But this little voice would not leave me alone. So, I decided to do it. I decided to really listen to the voice. I don't know why it took me so long to really listen, but I knew I needed to do *something*. I couldn't keep going with the heavy burden I felt. I didn't want God not to forgive me when I needed to be forgiven. So, I had to forgive. I had to forgive Tony.

And I did. I forgave him on my knees, crying to the Lord. I cried so hard and so long that I finally heard the Lord say,

"That's enough." But I didn't stop. No. I kept crying and being angry. I cried so hard asking Him why He did what He did and just didn't take her husband instead. Next thing I knew I couldn't breathe; I was gasping for air and I could not breathe. The voice said again—a little more insistently—"enough."

You can bet I stopped crying then and said I forgave her husband.

I forgave him but I wasn't perfect. I'm human. I still felt myself getting angry when anyone mentioned his name, but in time, the hardness faded. In 2013, Tony came to my house and thanked me for all I had done for him by helping D'Ana and him through some rough times. Mostly when I took guardianship of the fourteen-year-old son he had with D'Ana when Tony couldn't take care of him and raised him as my own.

The sad irony is that Tony too suffered an aneurysm. He survived and became thankful to God for saving him. Hearing that, peace washed over me.

Maybe that was what I was holding out for, at least subconsciously. I needed to see him in person so I could really let it go. Doing so taught me something really important; sometimes your mind forgives, but it takes time for the heart to catch up.

BELINDA
I Loved Idell Nivens, Why Did She Have to Die?

I loved her. Only 5'5" but a tower of strength. Copper brown complexion with long, soft, black hair hanging just below her shoulders. Hair that, when she was younger, fell to her waist. When she went out, she would often grab a short, sassy wig.

Looking at her medium frame, full on top and full in the middle, she would joke that she was pregnant. Around the house, she was casual. But when she got ready to go out, she got quite glamorous.

Her personality was as captivating as her looks. She could engage anyone in a deep conversation. She was quick to empathize and quick to laugh. It was impossible not to enjoy being in her company. She was quick to give encouragement, lend an ear or, when needed, give advice.

We lived in the same home, a three-floor, three-bedroom townhouse located in a middle-class, family-friendly neighborhood in Baltimore, Maryland. We had a small garden with a rose bush and walk that came up to our porch, where we could sit on warm days.

When you came into the house, you walked into the living room. As soon as you came in, you came face-to-face with an artificial, white fireplace. One of the walls had been a canvas for a local artist to paint an abstract vision. A gold coat rack stood between two huge boulders that had been in the house when we purchased it. They were too heavy to lift so they became part of the décor. Most of the furniture was conservative but the features like the rocks, the abstract, and miniblinds gave it a modern appeal.

It was a comfortable house, with a coffee table where the Bible rested close by to anyone sitting or lying on the couch.

Everything, from the furniture to the small touches, was in its place. Orderly. Just like her. She was very special and dear to me. She was the one who encouraged me when I was low. She listened to me when I bemoaned things that didn't go as planned. She cared for me through colds, fevers, and summer allergies. If I locked my keys in the car, she was the one to come to my rescue. She was friendly but could also be strict. She believed that kids needed to come in when the streetlights came on. Requests to go out on dates were often met with a firm, "no."

She thought of me when she was out shopping. She always brought something for me. She cooked special dinners at holiday times and guests were treated like family.

I watched her reach out to others in love. Sons- and daughters-in-law were family and were treated as such.

* * *

She had been a kidney patient for about eight years without complaint. In fact, we didn't even know anything was wrong. She was patient and determined. Her husband was happy to take care of her but she still got up every morning for work. If nothing else, she wanted some extra spending money for her grandchildren and foster children.

When my dad had health issues, she took care of him, making sure he made his doctor appointments and got his prescriptions filled.

She was a wife, a sister, and an aunt. But for me, she was my mother, caring for me and my family.

Later in life, she got her license to be a daycare provider. Once again, she was caring for others. She made sure that the children were clean and well-fed. When parents came to pick up their children, they would end up sitting and talking for hours. I can hardly count the times when I wanted them to leave so that I could talk with my mother, but she would never think of hurrying anyone on. God gave her something and people loved to be in her presence. So, I shared her with parents, postal workers, her club members, and nearly everyone that she came in contact with.

Sunday mornings were filled with the sound of gospel music and the smell of a hot breakfast. She would attend the eight o'clock service at Central Baptist Church and then come home, change her clothes, and start cooking. Every day was a power-packed day. She went on shopping sprees. She went on trips with the church. She went to club events. Some people move through life passively. She lived it.

When my brother passed away, my parents were hit hard. Although at times quiet, I never saw either of them cry. She was a very strong woman, a real Christian soldier.

One day, she came home from the doctor and she let us know that there was a problem with one of her kidneys, that she may need dialysis. This hit me like a ton of bricks. I prayed, and I know she prayed. Still, we did not spend a great deal of time discussing her health. The changes that were taking place in her body did not stop her from being who she was. Taking care of herself was like another assignment or job. Three days a week, she went to dialysis. When she did, one of her friends came in as back up and looked after her daycare children. Then she would come home from dialysis, feed the children, and carry on as if nothing had happened.

On Saturday mornings, she would get up early and go to the slaughterhouse for meats for the week. She would come home and put away whatever was purchased and then she would go to the supermarket and come home and put those things away. Then she would get ready for one of my sisters to come and take her out shopping. Friday and Saturday nights, she and I would look at movies that were rented from the video store.

Everything was planned around dialysis. She never let it hold her back.

One of the things she was committed to was being an usher at Central Baptist Church under the pastorship of the late Dr. Montague Brackett. When she ushered, she would put on her white uniform and be ready for service. That was her life, service. She showed love and she handled pain silently.

The daycare children called her "Momma." Her grandchildren called her "Momma." She was my mother and with all of the love we had, we called her Momma. She was the one I could talk to. She was the one who would understand. She was the one who shared quiet times, holidays, summer breezes, and stories of yesterday.

* * *

One day while watching television, she was lying at the foot of her bed and I looked over at her. My heart felt heavy. Once, long before, I'd told her that I didn't know what I'd do if anything ever happened to her. I repeated it then. She told me not to say that. I respected her wishes and proceeded to watch television.

But that day could not help but come. I was up early to leave for work. We talked briefly before I left. She was still in bed. I remember being frustrated with some of the plans for my wedding dress. I was making plans and discussing the veil that I wanted to wear.

She said not to worry about it. How could I know that while I focused on my wedding plans, other plans were already in motion? I believe I kissed her goodbye and left for work.

It was raining hard when I got off work. To me, something didn't feel right. I could feel my grip tightening on the handle of the seat in front of me. When we arrived at one of the park-and-ride stops, I saw my sister's boyfriend there. This was a strange occurrence. I was anxious when I got off the van.

"Hey," I said.

He said, "Hey," back.

Maybe it was a coincidence but no, he was there for me. "Is something wrong?" I asked, trying to keep my voice strong.

"I'll let your sister tell you," he said simply.

Anxious as I was, I decided I'd assume they were planning a bridal shower surprise or something. But then, he didn't take me home. He took me over to my sister's house.

There, I was told that my mother was in the hospital. Something serious was wrong. My first thought was, Why did they let me work all day without telling me? I could have taken the van home or driven my own car. But now I had to wait for someone to take me to the hospital to see her.

"She'll be all right," I told myself. She is strong. Really strong.

I cried and worried the next seven days, seven days that felt like I was suspended in air. Seven days of waiting. She wasn't able to talk. All she could do was lay there, helpless, but I was the one who felt helpless.

Those days were difficult. Still, I had to believe that she would get better.

At that time, my uncle, her brother, was living with us. One night, when he was on the phone, I heard him tell whomever he was talking to hold on, that another call was coming through. His eyes widened. He looked at me. "Get dressed," he said. "We have to get to the hospital."

I hurried to dress. My heart felt like it was skipping beats. The ride, like everything else during those days, seemed endless. "Hurry," I cried out. But he drove slow and steady, like he was in a funeral procession.

When we got to the hospital, we were told that she was gone. Gone.

I don't remember the next moments or hours clearly. Nothing felt real. It was like living in a nightmare. Everything was the same, but nothing was the same. The house was lonely and still. I was devastated.

I didn't know how to live in the house anymore.

The smell of perfume was in her room, but she was not. The house that was filled with love was now gray. The frame, mortar, and bricks were there, but the warmth had dissipated. Everything familiar to me felt strange. The refuge of home became an empty house of tears and pain.

She was no longer in the kitchen when I came home from work. Her voice was gone. So was her laughter. Everything was in the past. All my future dreams were changed. I wanted her to see me get married. I wanted to see her again. I wanted to hear her voice. I wanted to share my joys with her.

I felt there was too much death. My dad had passed away. My brother was gone. I couldn't believe this was happening again. My mother, the one who held it all together, was gone. She would not be coming back.

Her natural eyes never saw me get married. She wasn't around to see my children born. She was no longer there for me to discuss a dilemma or share a joy. I was so elated when each child was born, even so, there was also a melancholy, a sadness. I wanted to share my joys with someone who meant so much to me.

I have come to understand the quiet calm in her. I never saw her cry, but I saw moments of quiet calm. My parents were special. My mother meant so much to me.

It was painful losing her and it was also selfish of me to want to keep her here, knowing that her physical body was failing. I loved her and it took me a long time to forgive her for leaving. It wasn't easy to forgive because I couldn't see past my own pain. To forgive her meant I had to stop thinking about me and think of her. Once I shifted my focus and set my eyes to the hills from whence cometh my help, according to the Holy Scriptures, then I was able to realize the magnitude of being able to be with Jesus!

I thought to myself, who in their right mind would turn that down? How selfish I was. At first, I would feel sad and then hurt and then I would try not to feel anything at all. I know we are all but passing through this place called earth. We were never meant to stay here. I wanted to keep my mother here. I wanted to keep my loved ones with me. If I had my way, she and my dad would still be here. My brothers and sisters and I would always be together. But my plan is not greater than God's plans.

I cried many nights before this really hit me. There were times when I would hear my mother's voice calling me, only to wake up to silence. I was on an emotional rollercoaster. I was and am a Christian. I didn't expect to mourn like this. I knew who she was, but I had to remember who I was. I am a Christian. But I was lost in grief.

I am a child of the most high God. Mary must have suffered when Jesus was taken away. No one is exempt from pain. There are times that we must be still and allow God to do what he knows is best. We don't have to comprehend but we do need to trust Him. I knew this but I couldn't carry the pain any longer. I had to give it over to Him. I didn't want to feel any more pain. It was too great to keep reliving. I could not forget someone that meant so much, and I wasn't sure I wanted to. It was painful to remember. I had to hand it over to God.

I believed I would see her again but that did not relieve me of the pain until I attempted to give it to God. I had to pray about it. I had to leave it there. Which meant that I had to stop pondering over what I didn't have and consider what I did have. God permitted me to mourn and then He gave me the strength to lift up my head.

I read from the Holy Bible in that house we both lived in. It is recorded in the Scriptures that Jesus would be with me always. I stopped focusing on the lost and began to focus on Him. Jesus is bigger than any situation that we can possibly go through. He is bigger than any storm that we can imagine. It is okay to mourn but there is a time to cease mourning. There is a time and a season for everything, according to Ecclesiastes 3:1 NIV: "There is a time for everything, and a season for every activity under the heavens."

We all must go through some things, but it is better to go through them with Jesus than without Him. I had shared her with so many when she was here. I was reminded that God shared her with me. I have a relationship with God. I have Him in my life. I am not alone. I do not have to hold on to this pain any longer.

I know that Jesus said to, "Cast all your anxiety on him because he cares for you" (I Peter 5:7 NIV). I found solace in that. I am a Christian and she was also. I believe the Holy Spirit began to minister to me. The Holy Spirit is able to bring things back to our remembrance. Read, study, and learn the Scriptures. It is easier to bring back to your remembrance what you have been exposed to. I had to be still. I had to stop crying long enough to hear. Consider Psalms 46:10 where God tells us to be still and know that he is God, or John 15:4 in the Holy Scriptures, where we are told to abide in Him, and He will abide in us. There are sixty-six books in the Bible. There is so much knowledge, wisdom, and love in the Bible. Scriptures that I had read in the past began to surface for me. The recall was heard like a voice in my mind and heart. I believe she is in a better place.

Now I can recall pleasant memories without the pain that used to make me feel like time was standing still. Now the memories are like melodies. I can smile when I think of her. I can tell my children about her. I can remember when we were small and she would sing songs with us. We would record them and listen. My children have heard stories about my mother. I have been able to show them the old photo albums. Jesus said, "The thief does not come except to steal, and to kill, and to destroy. I have come that they may have life, and that they may have it more abundantly," John 10:10 (NKJV). This informs me that he wants us to have life.

I believe we should enjoy the life that we have, while we have it. We have been given opportunities to form wonderful relationships. There is one relationship that supersedes all others. I can tell you about my mother. I was there with her. This reminds me of others who were with someone special before He left. Yes, the disciples were with Jesus.

I am not comparing my mother to Jesus. I do want to show that there were those who walked with Him. There were those who saw firsthand and their information has been documented even as I share my story. His story is great and has an impact on each of us.

I hope that my story has touched you in some way. Even more, I hope that you are moved to read *His* story. I hope that my story will cause you to think. His story can change your life. God has been gracious to allow us to come in contact with special people. I am grateful for the family that I was born into. I feel blessed to have walked along this journey with my mother. She was God's before she ever became mine. I believe she answered a call. No more pain, no more sorrow, no more dialysis, no more trips to the hospital. No suffering. No tears.

My eyes were opened, and I was allowed to see it from a different perspective. I loved her, yet I had to realize that God loved her first. I loved her and my love was great. His love was even greater. He died for her, me, and all who are reading this and more. He knew her before I did. He loaned her to me for many years and then I believe he called her home. I realized that I had to forgive her. I was angry that she had left. I love her and I want the best for her. She would want the best for me. I believe that she has gone to a better place.

We are taught through Scripture to forgive, and once I was able to do this the pain of loss began to gradually subside. Holding on to unforgiveness is like holding on to something very hot. It is painful. We need to release it. We need to forgive. Sometimes, we are able to tell the person that we forgive them and then there are times when that person may not be around to hear it audibly. It is still necessary for us to forgive and let go. You can allow God to assist you. Pray. He is a prayer away. He can assist by providing a peace. We are able to go to God and ask His forgiveness for things that we have done wrong. He is merciful. It starts with us making up our minds to do it. Take the first step and forgive that one who has wronged you. There's a scripture that says, "If you love Me, keep my commandments" (John 14:15 NKJV). It got me thinking. If I love my mother as I say I do, then I will understand. Would I like to go to a better place? Would I like to one day be with Jesus? Would I want to endure the symptoms of illness in my body for long periods of time? Do I want what's best for my loved ones? Who knows best or more than God? My trust was and is in Him. I forgave her and I let go, knowing that she raised me, loved me, shared and left many precious memories with me. I have been blessed to have the ones that I hold dear. I thank God for my mother. I thank Him for times that He permitted us to share. Now I am a mom. I thank Him for my family. I once didn't know what I would do, but later I learned what I would have to do and that was to forgive.

Knowing and believing that she is in a better place was a good thing, but it was God's prescription of forgiveness that allowed me to let go of the pain and give it all to God. Forgiveness brought me the freedom to move forward. All thanks be to God.

ROSE
He Violated Me...I Bounced From Home to Home

My four siblings and I lived in Arkansas. Other than the number of my siblings, there wasn't much about my childhood that stood out. My memories of my dad stand out. I was three when he died, and to this day, I remember him in many ways. He had a light brown complexion, dreamy-sleepy eyes, chiseled high cheek bones, rather tall, over six feet, and very handsome.

I remember how he would come home, and I would always get into his pockets looking for pennies. Then, I thought pennies were worth more than silver. Or I would hop up onto his back for a ride. Dad called me his rainbow baby; that's a baby that comes after the death of a child. On December 5, 1953, when I was born, our family had four children but had also lost two—a brother to leukemia, and a sister died a crib death at three months. Two of us survived. But not until after Mom couldn't bear children for thirteen years. Those were long, praying years; years praying that God would have favor on Mom to have children, although the doctor felt she shouldn't conceive.

I was Dad's favorite. He loved me so much that whatever I asked for he gave me, like the TV my brothers put me up to asking him for. He said, "Baby, whatever you want, Daddy will get for you." Dad would put me in front of the TV and say, "This is your TV."

I was too young to understand much about my dad's death. Most of what I remember, I remember about my mom. I'll call her Sarah for this story. She was tall like Dad, about 5'9"; slim and shapely. She was beautiful and loved to dress so her lipstick matched. Every dress she wore was starched to perfection.

She worked her life doing day work for two families, caring for them like those in the movie, *The Help*.

I loved and revered Mom. She was a disciplinarian who carried switches to keep us in line, but she took no pleasure in doing so. She would rather play games with us or watch a movie like *The Wizard of Oz* together.

Like so many women carrying too much of a load, she had blood pressure and other health issues, but she couldn't be slowed by those. She pushed through life and worked to keep our family afloat.

March 9, 1962. I was only eight years old when Mom took ill. I waited anxious out of my mind with my family for the ambulance to get her. On her way to the hospital she died from a heart attack. She was only forty-two.

I was sure she would be coming home. She was strong. Strong as an ox. She'd overcome Dad's death. I just knew she'd overcome the heart attack.

At the funeral, people were wailing but I said, "Why are they crying? She's coming back home." They would shun me, but I was sure she'd come back.

But she did not come back. I was left with a void in my heart. From the time the ambulance came for her, I clutched her purse tight to my chest and held it. We were planning to go shopping before she took ill.

Letting that purse go meant she was really gone.

My mom's sister and husband took care of me, but they weren't used to children, so Mom's niece who was close to Mom (my first cousin on my mom's side) came one Sunday to get me to live with her and her family.

She was very nice, fair skin, beautiful with four children. With me in the house, five. I was received into this new family with open arms; I was happy. The kids welcomed me as their sister. I called them Mom and Dad.

Mom had a baby in diapers, so I helped wash and hang the clothes on the line before school. I helped with other chores, like the dishes. I fit in with the family. But then things started to change when I was around twelve and I got my period and started to develop. The man who I called Dad and loved as a dad started talking inappropriately sexually, about doing things to me. Developing scared me so much, yet I was a feisty girl, and would fight anyone, yet he continued.

One day, I was washing dishes alone. Mom was at the store with the kids. He started talking. I told him to stop and leave me alone. But that day, he was in a real talkative mood. He moved close to me. Too close. I grabbed a knife. Although he never touched me, I gave him a warning. "If you don't leave me alone, I will stick this knife in you." I was scared of him and I hated him. I cried whenever I was alone and he was around.

He snorted. "You're crazy..."

"I'm your daughter, you shouldn't be acting like this toward me," I told him.

I wanted to tell Mom what was happening but she was old school, the way she waited on him. I couldn't tell her. I didn't know what to do. He kept up his behavior until finally I couldn't bear it anymore and I told her.

Thank God she believed me. She talked to him. He stopped. He considered himself as God's gift to women. He was dark, so dark he was like dark blue, known for philandering and having other girls on the side. He even had a baby out of wedlock.

One summer, I travelled to my aunt and uncle's—my mom's biological brother—in Buffalo, New York. Before the visit ended, I sat down with my uncle and told him about what was going on with my dad. He got angry, I mean really angry. He called my mom and told her to put my dad on the phone. He challenged him about what I'd said. Dad admitted it.

"I want all of her stuff boxed up now and sent. She's not coming back."

In Buffalo, I had a good life. No stress. His wife was real bossy, maybe because she was going through menopause. She was evil to me and my uncle. After a while, I went back to Arkansas where I lived with my father's sister for a short time. My uncle sent me there because his wife was emotionally abusive. Then I went to Michigan during the fall of 1971 to be with my biological brother. He wanted to take care of me. It was a wonderful time of unification for us. He was four years older and became my anchor. I was also able to help his wife and family with responsibilities.

By this time, I was in the twelfth grade. I was able to complete a year of college.

All this disruption and moving from one family to another and changes I've had to adapt to was all because of how the man I called Dad treated me. My biggest challenge has been the unforgiveness I've had toward him.

I'm now sixty-one years old. Two years ago, in the year leading up to my retirement, God spoke to me and told me I had to forgive him. For forty-six years, I had carried such hate for him. I didn't want to hear his name, his laugh, or anything about his family. When my girls were born, I didn't want them to be around him, not for an hour or a minute. When he came to visit his family, I wouldn't let him stay with my family. I would allow Mom to stay with us. She wasn't the problem. That's how much I disdained this man I called Dad.

I told the Lord I wanted Him to use me to build up the Kingdom. I told Him whatever He wanted me to do I was open to doing. I desired my heart to be like God's heart.

He called me to give out Christian books to churches. But I had an awakening in my quiet moments praying by my bedside. The Lord told me before I could be assigned this project, I had to forgive my dad.

I told Him, I loved everyone. But God brought his name up. "Before you can be like me, you must forgive." We had a dialogue going.

I said, "You know how he hurt me?"

The Lord said, "You need to forgive. You can't work with people if you don't forgive him." He said, "I want to love on him like I would your biological father for the rest of your days."

It was the most challenging order I'd ever received when communing with the Lord. From that day to this one, He would remind me, "This is your daddy." So, on Father's Day, Christmas, and other special days, I begin to honor my father because the Word tells me to.

I can assure you; it wasn't me, but God.

Forgiveness doesn't come at one time; it's a gradual thing. When you have a close walk with the Lord, He will guide you on how to forgive. I began a daily walk with Him when I was eight years old, why not continue to listen to His voice to begin the journey of forgiveness. I can say, I've forgiven my father for everything.

So, the Lord spoke to me to give tracts everywhere I go. They're titled, "One minute after you die."

Now, God is using me for a wonderful ministry for the Kingdom. If I would not have forgiven Dad, God would not have used me for His ministry work, which I enjoy so much.

"For God so loved the world that He gave His only begotten son, that whoever believes in Him should not perish but have everlasting life" (John 3:16 NKJV). If He loved me so much to die for me to have everlasting life, I can forgive my father and love him.

VANESSA
Learning to Forgive My Dad Who Lived Two Lives

My name is Vanessa R. I am twenty-one years old and this is my story of forgiveness. We all struggle in our lives. Over the past four years, I have had to overcome a lot.

I was raised by wonderful parents who taught me right from wrong. I was taught to respect others and to treat them the way I wanted to be treated. I never was in trouble or disrespected my parents. I was lucky. I had a good family and a good home. I considered myself a good daughter.

My dad worked construction and provided well for us. I never needed anything. I grew up in San Pedro, California, for the first fifteen years of my life. I have one sister, Jen, who is three years younger than me.

Around the summer of 2010 things began to change. My dad bought a home in Wilmington, California. What I thought was a perfect relationship between my mom and dad turned out not to be so perfect. I found out how "not so perfect" one day when I was at home with some cousins. We were all in the living room when there was a knock on the door. I opened it and there stood a woman.

"Does Tony live here?"

"That's my dad. Can I help you with something?"

She looked confused for a second and said, "He has been living with me, I am three months pregnant." I was speechless! As soon as the woman left, I called my mother at her best friend's house in Long Beach. I assumed that everything the woman said was true. My dad was a liar and he was living two separate lives. Even so, I didn't want to believe it because he was my role model, a hard worker, provider for the family. I looked up to Dad. I wanted to be like him when I grew up.

After that afternoon, things with my parents just fell apart. My dad didn't want anything to do with my mother. He was in love with this other woman who, in my opinion, had nothing to offer him. I didn't just make it up either. I learned it from her own mouth.

After she came to our house, my mom talked to the woman. When she got to the house, Mom told her to hide herself in the closet. When she looked alarmed, Mom just told her to trust her. Soon, Dad arrived. My mom had a serious talk with Dad. He didn't say he loved the other woman at first but, after a time, he did. He told her they met at a bar. She already had four kids with three different men. It seemed that she just wanted everything we had as a family. And, she was jealous. She kept Dad from me and my sister. Over time, his affection drifted from us girls toward this woman.

You can bet I felt betrayed.

I don't think either my mom or dad realized how their failing relationship affected my sister and me. We had our house, a brand-new Range Rover, what we called a "good" life. And then it was just snatched from us.

We had four cars. One by one, he started taking them away. He didn't give Mom a car for work, or couldn't take us to school. My dad had a steady job with money. He became greedy and threw us out of the house, telling Mom that he couldn't pay for the house because the economy was bad. He said he wasn't working much at the time and that he lost the house in foreclosure.

He told us we had to be out in two weeks.

He lied.

We later learned that he rented it out.

Dad's family sided with him. Mom said fighting wasn't worth it. She said saying something wouldn't make it better.

I was angry and hurting inside. I stopped caring about the things I'd always cared about. I stopped going to school. At sixteen, with all my anger and the chaos in my life, I started to drink. I just wanted to drink the emotional pain away. I was drinking vodka. I know I was wrong but without anyone to talk to, I needed to numb the pain.

Then I began to cut, not deep, but I was a cutter. I felt driven by the anger I had toward my father. I wanted attention from him and from Mom. Mom had her own way of dealing with her pain. She would lock herself in her room and didn't want to hear about our issues.

My mother never raised her voice. She was sweet and caring with beautiful soft brown hair. She was raised by her father with four siblings. She came from Mexico. She never got into trouble.

At the time all this was happening, she was about thirty-six, neat and well-organized with a clean and tidy house. She showed me how to look after myself. If we made a mess, we had to clean it up. She told us that everything had a place.

I don't know why, but my dad's side of the family never liked her. It was easy for them to turn against her and us when all this happened. They thought my dad was this innocent man when in reality he was the one cheating on my mom, even hitting her. I didn't understand domestic violence back then, because my sister and I stayed in my room. It had been going on for a time. My dad drank a lot and when he would come to the house, he would just pick a fight with my mother. It just never ended.

One time, the cops arrested Dad when I was home and he went to jail for domestic violence. But I had questions—Why is this happening to my mom? She's nice, why? I didn't think it was right. I was young and didn't know what to do. Oh yes, there was domestic violence, with their divorce and a mistress with a baby on the way. Cop cars pulled up at the house. If it was not one thing, it was another. I hated my dad with all my heart because of this woman and what he had done to my mom, my sister, and me. He wasn't around, his attention was on another woman and a new baby.

My mom struggled to start fresh. She got a new place of her own. She worked to make her way. It was hard for her but she did it. Today, I'm proud of her for being the strong woman that she was, and showed us how to be.

Things started to look up for Mom but everything for my dad went downhill. His girlfriend had a boy, so I now had a baby brother. But other than that, things were bad. Turned out that the mother of his child was crazy. My dad thought he would have a happy ending but he was in and out of jail because of his girlfriend.

This was the year that was most difficult for me. I realized I had to do something with my life and make my family proud. I never had that connection with my mother as most other people do. Here I was, a drop-out, and I decided to go back to school and go into a trade to become a medical assistant. I saw a lot of commercials for Everett College, so in 2012, I began college in the medical assistant program. I wanted to make Mom proud. I actually did accomplish something. Two months into the program, I found out that I was pregnant. My daughter was born on November 28, 2012.

I didn't want to tell anybody. Not my mom. Not my dad. The father of my child was not in the picture. He didn't even believe me when I told him it was his child.

Slowly, as time passed, I began to forgive my dad. A gentle voice inside told me it wasn't good to hold a grudge forever. So, I decided to focus on forgiving him. Being angry and resentful didn't make me happy. It didn't solve anything. I began to write to him. I told him how he put us through a lot; how it was hurtful with the other woman.

I became pregnant with a second child, a son. My son's grandmother took me to Cornerstone Christian Center Church in Torrance. There, my faith in Christ grew. There were a lot of bad days, days when I despaired, days when I felt as low as I could imagine. But attending church made me feel good about myself. I was in a better place. I understood that if I was ever going to be happy with myself, I would need to let go of everything.

So, I forgave my dad, but I did not forget.

A month before I gave birth, I wrote to him and told him my situation. He told me he supported me. It made me feel good, but I had yet to tell my mother.

It was hard to tell her. I knew she had problems of her own. But I knew I had to tell her. I wrote a letter to her and told her. She made clear that it wouldn't be easy but accepted it like my dad. Since that time, so much has changed. I have a different mindset now. I view myself as a mature twenty-one-year-old.

I've learned a lot through these experiences. I've learned that no matter what you go through in life, negative situations will not always stay that way. Believe in God. Be happy with yourself. Help others and never judge a book by its cover. Make every second of your life count because life is short, and you should appreciate everything you have in life.

If you consider your life and look at those who are less fortunate, then you'll have greater appreciation for your life. I know firsthand because I once had nothing. I am in a good place now; more independent and working to help out my mom with what I can. I've never been so happy and grateful for everyone in my life. In 2015, I gave birth to a son who has brought a lot of happiness to my life. My dad was released from prison the following year, in 2016. He finally came to the realization that his girlfriend wasn't good for him, and he told her it was over.

Sadly, that same year, my mom was on drugs. In March 2016, she took her life. I struggled and grieved with her death. It set me back emotionally. Once again, I became homeless and ended up in a shelter with my baby.

Finally, in October 2017, I began working and my life began turning around. The great lesson learned was finally getting learned—we all go through difficult times. Things were pretty bleak for a while, but I didn't give up. I struggled before and made it. I can do it again. I have people who love and support me. God has helped me get through the difficult times.

When I feel overwhelmed and wonder why I want to live, I think of my kids. I don't want them to live without me. I want them to have me. They are my motivation. Without them, and God in my life, I wouldn't be here.

PAUL
Hating My Mom...
Loving My Mom

January of 1985. The night before, I had been with Frances, a friend of mine. I had a drink in one hand and a cigarette in the other. I paused and looked at myself. Man, I thought to myself, there's got to be more to life than this. Now, I was driving from Sacramento to our Bay Area office when I felt compelled to pull off North Texas Road in Fairfield and stop my car. I climbed over the barbed wire fence along the road and climbed a steep hill. At the top of the hill, I met God at a lone oak tree and everything changed.

Not long after, I was visiting my brother, Steve. We got along fine. Not long after I arrived, he got a call. He said Theodora, our sister, needed a ride. No problem. What I didn't know was that we were picking her up at a café frequented by pimps, prostitutes, and junkies. Oh, and as it turned out, my mother worked there.

* * *

Sixteen years earlier, when I was twelve, I told my mother I hoped she died and that I never wanted to see her again. That might seem harsh but she had abandoned six children for a man who pimped her. Before she left, our parents sent us to their friend's home. I did not want to stay there. I sneaked back home through my bedroom window. I walked out into the living room where my father was passed out drunk and naked on the sofa. I heard talking going on in their bedroom which was across from my room. I slipped under the bed in my room and saw my mother and Charles come out naked. I ran from the house as quick as I could, crazy mad. That night, I slept in the backyard, refusing to have anything to do with them. I wished them all dead.

Suddenly, arguing broke out. My mother screamed, "Go to … I am leaving and never coming back!" At that moment, the front door slammed. I started crying because I knew, being the oldest, I would be responsible for my siblings and I would be beaten more by an angry drunk. Shortly after my mother left, my father began beating me. One night I told him the next time he hit me I would kill him. I knew I could and would, so right after saying it that night, I walked from Stockton to Tracy along Highway 5. I never went back. My father died at fifty-seven.

* * *

I did not want to go in to the café. I still had unforgiveness in my heart toward her. I sat in my car, waiting for Steve to return with our sister. It was then that I sensed God telling me to go in and forgive her. I was a young man, only twenty-eight years old. I was spending a lot of time in prayer and reading Scripture. At that moment, in my car, God's words seemed to come alive in me, changing me, convicting me and compelling me to love, accept, and forgive. In doing so, I was the one being healed.

I went in the café.

I would have recognized her with my eyes closed. I heard her voice. She had her back to me, talking to two transgenders at a booth. I walked up to the booth. She turned and looked at me. She did not recognize me.

"Hi, Helen. It's Paul."

"This is my son!" she cried out. Her voice was both sad and glad, surprised and subdued. She moved over so I could sit. I told her about my experience with God and how I needed to ask her to forgive me for hating her for abandoning us.

She wept uncontrollably. She hugged me, and I hugged her back. She was only forty-nine, but the hardships of her life had made her old. She was wearing a tattered black dress. She was overweight. Her hair was black, straight, and uncombed.

As I shared with them about Christ, Helen, my mother, pulled a crumpled piece of paper out of her purse. It was the song "How Great Thou Art." We sang that song together in the café, and she sung with an angelic voice! This was truly a divine encounter.

I spent the next six months, six days a week, visiting her and customers at the café every night after work, sharing God's love and His Word. Her pay for working there was her meals. She lived on a widow's pension and Social Security, barely

$600.00 per month. Her room at the hotel was $140.00. With the balance, she helped her friends on the street.

She was a giver.

I shared the Word of God with everyone in the café. At the same time, I told my mother I would move her to Lodi to be close to my home and the church I'm involved with. I wanted her out of that place. So, I kept coming and sharing, trying to convince her to leave, until one evening God's Spirit spoke to me and said, "Love and accept her where she is, trust me."

After that, I no longer asked her to come closer to me. I just kept coming back befriending and loving those who were there. Miracles were happening, deliverance and restoration. I prayed for people and soon after, people began quitting drugs and prostitution. God taught me to love and accept people for who they are, not for what they have done. If you were to ask me what did God do to make this transformation in my life from rejecting my mother to accepting her, I would have to say it is in His calling of me to serve Him.

God has taught me in order to love others, one must love God, self, and when that miracle of transformation takes place, you can freely love others.

Six months. Six months of witness.

Six months after reuniting with my mother, she fell and went into a coma and never recovered. Seven days later, she walked into Heaven. Three months after that, September 1985, I entered a Bible college. I am reminded of that day when we sang that song, written by Carl Boberg in 1885. Whenever I hear it, my soul is filled with joy, for I know my faith is not a religion, it is defined by a personal relationship with Christ who is alive and real as you and me.

Verse 1
O Lord my God, when I in awesome wonder,
Consider all the worlds Thy hands have made;
I see the stars, I hear the rolling thunder,
Thy power throughout the universe displayed.

Chorus
Then sings my soul, my Savior God, to Thee,
How great Thou art! How great Thou art!
Then sings my soul, My Savior God, to Thee,
How great Thou art! How great Thou art!

Verse 2
When through the woods, and forest glades I wander,
And hear the birds sing sweetly in the trees.
When I look down, from lofty mountain grandeur
And see the brook, and feel the gentle breeze.

Chorus

Verse 3
And when I think, that God, His Son not sparing;
Sent Him to die, I scarce can take it in;
That on the cross, my burden gladly bearing,
He bled and died to take away my sin.

Chorus

Verse 4
When Christ shall come, with shout of acclamation,
And take me home, what joy shall fill my heart.
Then I shall bow, in humble adoration,
And then proclaim, "My God, how great Thou art!"

Chorus

Afterword

The Woolstrum family at Century Youth Ranch, now known as Century Charities, had adopted Michael, my youngest brother. I have stayed connected and have a strong bond with Century Charities. They operate throughout California and other countries outside of the USA. He is founder and CEO of Touch International, Inc. in Texas. Today, he is a pastor, husband, father, and motivational speaker pursuing his doctorate. My sister Eva lived a life of drugs and sexual abuse. She came to the Faith Family Services ministry I started in Texas and has been delivered from drugs and has been growing as a follower of Christ since 2011. My other three siblings live in Stockton, California, and attend the Saint Basil Greek Orthodox Church in San Juan Capistrano, California.

Scriptures to Encourage Your Journey of Forgiveness

"Bear with each other and forgive one another if any of you has a grievance against someone. Forgive as the Lord forgave you" (Colossians 3:13 NIV).

"In prayer there is a connection between what God does and what you do. You can't get forgiveness from God, for instance, without also forgiving others. If you refuse to do your part, you cut yourself off from God's part" (Matthew 6:14 MSG).

"If we confess our sins, he is faithful and just and will forgive us our sins and purify us from all unrighteousness" (I John 1:9 NIV).

"And when you stand praying, if you hold anything against anyone, forgive them, so that your Father in heaven may forgive you your sins" (Mark 11:25 NIV).

"Instead of your shame you will receive a double portion, and instead of disgrace you will rejoice in your inheritance.
And so you will inherit a double portion in your land, and everlasting joy will be yours" (Isaiah 61:7 NIV).

"With your help I can advance against a troop; with my God I can scale a wall" (Psalms 18:29 NIV).

"I can do all things through Him who strengthens me" (Philippians 4:13 ESV).

"Lean on, trust in, and be confident in the Lord with all your heart and mind and do not rely on your own insight or understanding. In all your ways know, recognize, and acknowledge Him, and He will direct and make straight and plain your paths" (Proverbs 3:5-6 AMP).

"You have searched me, Lord, and you know me.
You know when I sit and when I rise; you perceive my thoughts from afar.
You discern my going out and my lying down; you are familiar with all my ways.
Before a word is on my tongue you, Lord, know it completely.
You hem me in behind and before, and you lay your hand upon me.
Such knowledge is too wonderful for me, too lofty for me to attain" (Psalm 139:1-6 NIV).

"Therefore, if anyone is in Christ, the new creation has come:
The old has gone, the new is here!"
(2 Corinthians 5:17 NIV).
"The Lord is my shepherd, I lack nothing.
He makes me lie down in green pastures,
he leads me beside quite waters, he refreshes my soul.
He guides me along the right paths for His name's sake.
Even though I walk through the darkest valley,
I will fear no evil, for you are with me;
Your rod and Your staff, they comfort me" (Psalm 23: 1-4 NIV).

"For God has not given us a spirit of fear, but of power and of
love and of a sound mind" (2 Timothy 1:7 (NKJV).

"But those who wait on the Lord shall renew their strength;
They shall mount up with wings like eagles,
They shall run and not be weary,
They shall walk and not faint" (Isaiah 40:31 NKJV).

"Now faith is the substance of things hoped for,
The evidence of things not seen" (Hebrews 11:1 NKJV).

"No weapon formed against you shall prosper,
And every tongue which rises against you in judgement
You shall condemn.
This is the heritage of the servants of the Lord,
And their righteousness is from Me,
Says the Lord" (Isaiah 54:17 NKJV).

"I will go before you and level the mountains; I will shatter the doors of bronze

And cut through the bars of iron" (Isaiah 45:2 NIV).

"If your enemies are hungry, give them food to eat. If they are thirsty,

give them water to drink. You will heap burning coals of shame on their heads,

and the Lord will reward you" (Proverbs 25:21-22 NLT).

"But Jesus looked at them and said, 'With men it is impossible, but not with God; for with God all things are possible" (Mark 10:27 NKJV).

"This is my command—be strong and courageous! Do not be afraid or discouraged. For the Lord your God is with you wherever you go" (Joshua 1:9 NLT).

A Prayer For Forgiveness

Father, thank you for your unconditional love for me.

I ask you to help me to forgive everyone who has hurt me, has dis-appointed me, betrayed me, abandoned me, caused me any harm, or people I have hurt.

Thank you for strength to let go of anger, bitterness, resentment, and any desire to pay them back. Now set me free from all the side effects of unforgiveness.

Father, I thank you that I can experience peace and joy that comes from you, in Jesus' name...Amen

Original Prayer by Eva Clark
Sister to Author, Co-Pastor, Musician

Endnotes

Introduction

1. Dr. Michael Barry, *Unforgiveness: A Disease That Can Be Treated*, HealthNewsDigest.com, (Philadelphia, PA, February 2011) 1, 2.

Chapter 3

2. Marvin's Story: Finding Courage to Forgive Through my Adoption. Adapted from Barker Adoption Foundation, Connections, *My Adoption Story*, Marvin Lynch, (Bethesda, MD, spring 2016), 6.

Chapter 6

3. Dr. Martin Luther King Jr., speaking throughout Mississippi, 1968, The Atlantic, *The Last March of Martin Luther King Jr.*, Drew Dellinger, (April 2018), www.theatlantic.com/politics/archive/2018/04/MLK-last .

Chapter 11

4. Gloria's Story: Breaking the Cycle of Sexual Molestation, Gloria Ewing Lockhart, *Unmasking A Woman's Journey*, A

Memoir of Courage, Hope, Forgiveness, and Healing, (Los Angeles, CA, 2012), 229.

5. Priscilla Shirer, Shirer's Quotes: 45 famous quotes about Shirer's, www.wisefamousquotes.com/quotes – about – Shirer; www.goingbeyond.com/ministry.

6. *The Journey: Forgiveness, Restorative Justice and Reconciliation, The Importance of Grieving and Facing Our Fears in the Journey of Reconciliation,* Stephanie Hixon and Thomas Porter, (New York, The United Methodist Church, Women's Division, The General Board of Global Ministries, 2011), 100.

7. Joyce Meyer, *16 Inspirational Joyce Meyer Quotes on Forgiveness,* #11 (www.joycemeyer.org) Joyce Meyer Ministries, St. Louis, Missouri.

8. Lewis B. Smedes Quotes, www.goodreads.com, author, *Forgive and Forget: Healing the Hurts We Don't Deserve,* (Harper Collins, 2007).

9. Top 25 quotes by Louis Zamperini, www.azquotes.com, author of several books, and movie, *Unbroken Louis Zamperini Story* (Laura Hillenbrand, 2014).

10. Johns Hopkins Medicine, Healthy Connections, *Forgiveness: Your Health Depends on It,* Karen Swartz, Psychiatry and Neurology, Johns Hopkins Hospital, www.hopkinsmedicine.org.

Glossary

Amplified Bible (AMP)
English Standard Version (ESV)
Good News Translation (GNT)
New International Version (NIV)
New King James Version (NKJV)
New Living Translation (NLT)
New Life Version (NLV)
The Message (MSG)

Spreading Forgiveness

Thank you for reading, *How Many Times Do I Forgive? Life-Changing Stories of People Who Have Chosen to Forgive.* You are invited to join a growing team of people who are encouraging others to forgive. I call this the Forgiveness Revolution. Here's how you can join us.

1. Recommend *How Many Times Do I Forgive? Life-Changing Stories of People Who Have Chosen to Forgive* to others and encourage them to tell others.
2. Leave a review on Amazon or with Trilogy Publishing Company about how much the book has impacted your life.
3. Drop me a line on FACEBOOK, www.facebook.com/gloria lockhart or email me at gloriaelockhart@gmail.com to share your successful forgiveness story or to make an inquiry.

"The Lord bless you and keep you;
the Lord make his face shine on you
and be gracious to you;
the Lord turn his face toward you
and give you peace" (Numbers 6:24-26 NIV).

CPSIA information can be obtained
at www.ICGtesting.com
Printed in the USA
FSHW010926310719
60556FS